Conspiracy Theories

Unsolved Mysteries, Murders, & Crimes

William S. Johnson

© Copyright 2021 by William S. Johnson. All right reserved.

The work contained herein has been produced with the intent to provide relevant knowledge and information on the topic described in the title for entertainment purposes only. While the author has gone to every extent to furnish up-to-date and true information, no claims can be made as to its accuracy or validity as the author has made no claims to be an expert on this topic. Notwithstanding, the reader is asked to do their own research and consult any subject matter experts they deem necessary to ensure the quality and accuracy of the material presented herein.

This statement is legally binding as deemed by the Committee of Publishers Association and the American Bar Association for the territory of the United States. Other jurisdictions may apply their own legal statutes. Any reproduction, transmission or copying of this material contained in this work without the express written consent of the copyright holder shall be deemed as a copyright violation as per the current legislation in force on the date of publishing and the subsequent time thereafter. All additional works derived from this material may be claimed by the holder of this copyright.

The data, depictions, events, descriptions, and all other information forthwith are considered to be true, fair, and accurate unless the work is expressly described as a work of fiction. Regardless of the nature of this work, the Publisher is exempt from any responsibility of actions taken by the reader in conjunction with this work. The Publisher acknowledges that the reader acts of their own accord and releases the author and Publisher of any responsibility for the observance of tips, advice, counsel, strategies, and techniques that may be offered in this volume.

Table of Contents

Table of Contents

Introduction

Chapter 1

Amy Lynn Bradley Disappeared in 1998

Chapter 2

Brian Schaffer, Disappeared in 2006

Chapter 3

Jodi Huisentruit, Disappeared in 1995

Chapter 4

Ben Needham, Disappeared in 1991

Chapter 5

Renata Antczak, Disappeared in 2017

Chapter 6

Rebecca Coriam, Disappeared in 2011

Chapter 7

The Incident at Dyatlov Pass

Chapter 8

The Flannan Isles Lighthouse Disappearances

Chapter 9

The Bridge at Overtoun That Calls Dogs to Their Maker

Chapter 10

The Voynich Manuscript

Chapter 11

The Mystifying Case of the Black Dahlia

Chapter 12

The Cleveland Torso Murderer

Chapter 13

The Infamous Hinterkaifeck Murders

Chapter 14

21st Century UFO Sightings

References

Introduction

Congratulations on purchasing *Conspiracy Theories,* and thank you for doing so.

There are plenty of books on this subject on the market. Thanks again for choosing this one! Every effort was made to ensure it is full of as much useful information as possible. Please enjoy!

Chapter 1
Amy Lynn Bradley Disappeared in 1998

The 1998 disappearance of Amy Lynn Bradley has grown so obscured in a vast web of corporate cover-ups, dead ends, scams, and criminal conspiracies that the basic facts of the case can often become lost in the noise. But, though theories abound, we must start at the beginning. On March 24, 1998, 23-year-old Amy Lynn Bradley was one of the thousands of passengers aboard the cruise ship *Rhapsody of the Seas*. She was onboard with her parents, Ron and Iva, and her brother, Brad. Her father had won cruise tickets for him and his wife from his employers, and the Bradleys elected to buy two additional tickets for their children. The ship—a standout vessel of the Royal Caribbean cruise line fleet—was about to dock at the Caribbean Island of Curaçao on the morning of March 23, scheduled for a daytime excursion before continuing on through the rest of its tour through the Caribbean.

According to her father's account, she was last seen (definitely, at least) in the early morning hours, possibly going out on their cabin deck for a smoke break, by her father as he woke briefly from sleep. Those, at the very least, are the facts as they are currently known.

After that, the only definitive fact is that Amy Lynn Bradley was never seen by her family again. Her father found her missing when he woke up later that morning and began what was at first a casual, somewhat annoying search for his erstwhile daughter. He assumed that she had no doubt simply wandered off to engage in some of the ship's various activities or perhaps continue flirting with a few of the crew's more handsome members, forgetting that the family had plans to deboard on Curaçao for the day. That search eventually grew more concerned and then outright desperate, as her parents and brother found no trace of

Bradley anywhere on the ship. By the middle of the day, the Bradley family was beginning to panic.

Among the most frustrating aspects of this case is how different Bradley's disappearance could have turned out had the ship's crew and corporate managers acted differently in the first crucial 48 hours following her disappearance. But, undoubtedly following a corporate protocol that prioritized damage control over passenger well-being, the ship's staff initially refused to seriously take reports of a missing passenger. While Bradley's parents reported their daughter missing to the ship's crew almost as soon as they began their search for her, the crew itself was initially dismissive of their concerns. They reassured the increasingly distraught family that their 23-year-old daughter had most likely wandered off to some wayward corner of the ship or possibly hooked up with a fellow passenger and was at that moment cloistered in another cabin, up to god knows what. More disturbingly, the crew initially refused to make any kind of ship-wide announcement of a missing passenger. Recalling the ordeal years later, Bradley's father noted that the staff seemed far more concerned with not disturbing the ship's other passengers or disrupting the ship's "party" vibe than they were with locating their missing daughter. When the crew finally *did* make a ship-wide announcement, it merely took the form of a vague request for Amy Bradley to report to the main cabin, made at a time when most of the passengers had already departed for their day trip to Curaçao. Now in an outright panic, the Bradley family eventually joined the rest of the passengers on Curaçao to see if their missing daughter had merely left without them. After several more hours of frantic searching turned up nothing, the Bradley family was forced to return to the *Rhapsody of the Seas* in another desperate attempt to get the ship's crew to take their daughter's disappearance seriously.

As the family now found, the good news was that the crew was, in fact, perhaps beginning to realize, at last, that Bradley's disappearance *may* be more serious than they had initially dismissed it as. The *bad* news was that the crew responded to this realization by contacting Royal Caribbean's legal department and informing the stricken Bradley family that they would not engage in any further communication without a company lawyer present. While the crew's initial response had been to prioritize the ship's "festive" atmosphere, it now seemed that their response had shifted to avoiding any and all legal liability.

Tragically for the Bradley family, more than 20 years later, these remain the only definitive facts about their daughter's disappearance. Though their lives have been consumed in a desperate search, all that they have so far uncovered have been unverified "sightings," webs of conspiracies and scams, stories of abductions, sex-trafficking rings, para-military operations, and potential coverups.

So, with these basic facts established, let's look at some of the theories regarding Amy Lynn Bradley's disappearance. The first and most fundamental theory (often proposed by those seeking to dismiss or quickly explain the case) is that Bradley simply fell or jumped from her family's cabin deck. She then drowned in the ocean and disappeared at sea—a fate shared by far too many others who go missing from cruise ships every year. However, while many have explored and advocated for this explanation, there are two significant issues. First, the specific design of the *Rhapsody of the Sea* includes barriers along its hull, separating individual cabin decks from the sea below. Thus, should a person have fallen from the cabin occupied by the Bradley family, it is far more likely that they would land on another deck or barrier below rather than fall directly into the ocean. Secondly, Bradley's parents have noted several times, as early as the day of her disappearance, that Bradley had a fear of water and a penchant for seasickness that had manifested itself earlier in the ship's voyage. Bradley would rarely wander too close to the edge of the vessel or lean too hard on a deck barrier. This was both to relieve her seaborn nausea and out of a fear of losing her balance and falling overboard. Bradley also had training as a lifeguard, making it even less likely that she would act so carelessly around water.

If Bradley did not, in fact, fall overboard the ship, either via an accident or by suicide, the prevailing theory that has taken hold in subsequent years is that she was the victim of a kidnapping plot of some kind. Here, things get somewhat murky, given the levels of speculation that have proliferated in the absence of any type of clear facts and given a few unconfirmed but heavily reported sightings. Shortly after her disappearance became a major news story, as her grief-stricken family became partial fixtures on news networks to make appeals for any information regarding their daughter's whereabouts, many amateur investigators began to connect Lynn's disappearance to whispered stories about intricate and sophisticated human tracking rings that supposedly operate throughout the Caribbean.

On a surface level, the notion that Bradley may have been kidnapped from a cruise ship, smuggled onto shore, and forced into prostitution *seems* a bit outlandish, more in line with Hollywood thrillers than anything that actually happened in real life. And, to be sure, there *are* numerous cases of actual human trafficking that occur every year across the Caribbean, Central America, and even the U.S. mainland. However, as pernicious as this issue is, human trafficking victims are most likely to be destitute and unknown women and children from extremely poor areas and vulnerable populations. In the vast majority of cases, human traffickers exploit already vulnerable migrants, orphans, and other groups who are least likely to attract any kind of attention from the authorities. To engage in a full-on abduction of an American tourist—from a cruise ship, no less—would be well outside the norm of how human traffickers operate, not least of all due to the extremely high risk of such a scheme well outweighing any potential benefits.

However, the theory that Bradley was in fact kidnapped by human traffickers has gained steam over the years as a result of several notable sightings, all of which, if verified, may show this theory to hold some weight. Of course, as with any high-profile missing person case, alleged sightings of Bradley poured into official networks almost immediately. However, while most of them can be dismissed fairly easily, authorities and the Bradley family themselves have identified three potential sightings as being at least somewhat credible. According to the Bradley, these theories lend credence to the theory that Amy is still alive but is being held captive in a human trafficking operation.

The first of these sightings came a few months after Bradley's initial disappearance. In August of 1998, two Canadian tourists in Curacao claimed that they saw a woman on a beach who bore a striking resemblance to Bradley. According to them, not only were the woman's face and hair the same as Bradley's, but she also had Bradley's distinctive tattoos and navel ring. The tourists also reported that this woman was being flanked by two men, who quickly ushered her away before either of the two Canadians could talk to her.

The second credible sighting occurred the following year. A United States Navy sailor who was on shore leave in Curacao claimed that he saw Bradley inside a brothel. According to him, she, upon seeing that he was a member of the U.S. armed forces, told him herself that her name was "Amy Bradley" and asked him for help. However, the woman was allegedly taken away before the sailor could do anything further. Unfortunately, out of a desire to hide the fact that he had been visiting a brothel, the sailor did not come forward with this information until more than a year later, long after the location he had been visiting had been shut down and well beyond the timeframe in which authorities could have potentially done anything.

The third and final supposed sighting occurred a few years later. In 2005, a woman named Judy Maurer claimed to have seen a woman bearing a striking resemblance to Bradley in a department store on the Caribbean island of Barbados. As with the account from the Canadian tourists, this woman was being flanked by a group of sketchy men, one of whom apparently threatened to beat her if she did not hold up her end of some unspoken "deal." Once the woman was by herself, Maurer claims that she took it upon herself to see if she was okay, at which point the woman told her that her name was "Amy" and that she was from Virginia. At this point in Maurer's story, the men returned and escorted "Amy" away before any more questions could be asked.

While all of these sightings may seem promising, they also come with their fair share of issues. For each to be believed, we must also believe that these supposed witnesses could not only recognize Bradley in person based on the limited pictures of her that they had seen but also recognize and recall a large number of minor details (including her tattoos and piercings) from nothing more than a quick, momentary glance. Then, of course, there's the additional complication that, since shortly after she first went missing, the Bradley family has been offering a reward of $250,000 for any information regarding Amy's whereabouts. This, unavoidably, raises the possibility of a financial motive for anyone who claims to have seen her, regardless of how credible their story is.

In 2005, the Bradley family received an anonymous email that contained a picture taken from a website advertising escort services in the Caribbean. The email focused on a picture of one particular escort who bore a noticeable resemblance to Bradley herself, albeit with a very different hairstyle. Going public with this image, the Bradleys have said that this verifies their theory that their daughter is, in fact, still alive, having been kidnapped from the ship and held in forced prostitution. However, the veracity of this image is somewhat questionable. Although an FBI facial recognition expert hired by the Bradleys did apparently give very high odds the photo did, in fact, portray their daughter, other investigations into the records of Caribbean escort services have potentially identified the woman in the picture as someone other than Bradley.

Chapter 2
Brian Schaffer, Disappeared in 2006

The 2006 disappearance of Brian Schaffer would be strange enough on its basic facts alone. After all, a promising, 27-year-old medical student suddenly going missing would likely have drawn some degree of national and international attention. But when you add the fact that Schaffer appears to have vanished *into thin air*, the case suddenly takes a much stranger turn.

In the Spring of 2006, Brian Schaffer was a 27-year-old student at Ohio State University Medical School in Columbus, Ohio. Though the life of an aspiring doctor is undoubtedly stressful, Schaffer was by all accounts relatively happy and optimistic about the future. For example, for the school's upcoming spring break, he and his girlfriend Alexis had booked a flight for a much-needed vacation to Miami, a trip that Brian, as far as anyone could tell, was quite looking forward to. Some friends and family members even believed that Brian was planning on using the trip to propose. On the surface, no one close to Schaffer would have any cause for concern or apprehension during the days leading up to April 1.

But, of course, that anticipated trip never happened. On the evening of March 31, the first day of Ohio State's Spring Break and a day before Brian and Alexis were scheduled to fly to Miami, he and a few friends went out drinking in downtown Columbus. Eventually, the group ended up at a bar known as the Ugly Tuna, located in a larger complex of bars and restaurants and something of a staple among the Columbus nightlight. More importantly, the Ugly Tuna also had several CCTV cameras trained on the bar's public entrances and exits, CCTV cameras that captured Brian and his friends entering the bar around midnight. Those same cameras later captured Brian talking to some women near the bar's front entrance before eventually going back inside, out of frame. This would, as it turned out, be the last image ever taken of Brian Schaffer.

When closing time rolled around at 2AM in the early morning of April 1, Brian's friends realized that they had lost track of him. When he failed to respond to any of their calls or texts, they assumed that he had merely left without them (possibly in anticipation of his later flight to Miami) and returned to their homes with little concern. However, the next day came, and Brian was still not responding to any attempt to contact him. Out of caution, his friends reached out to Brian's father, who had also not heard any word from his son since the previous evening. When Brian never showed up for his flight to Miami, his friends and family realized that the situation may be more serious than it had initially seemed. Now outright worried, Brian's family reported him missing to the Columbus Police Department. What they would find in their subsequent investigation would baffle experts and investigators to this day.

As the Ugly Tuna was the last location where Brian had been spotted, detectives got hold of the bar's CCTV footage from the night he went missing. The footage showed Brian and company entering the bar that evening, seemingly confirming his friends' account. Later, detectives saw the final footage of Brian talking to the young women in the building's lobby. But detectives then made a shocking revelation. Although the bar's CCTV footage showed Brian entering the bar, it never showed him *leaving*. Despite pouring over every second of footage from every camera trained on each of the bar's doors, and despite meticulously tracking the faces of everyone who entered and left the bar on the evening of his disappearance, investigators could find no sign of Brian ever leaving through any of the Ugly Tuna's exits, either of his own volition or someone else's. Based on this security footage, Brian, it seemed, had not merely *gone missing*. He appeared to have disappeared from reality entirely.

Thus, the mystery of Brian Schaffer's disappearance became not merely a question of *why* but also of *how*. At the time of Brian's disappearance, the Ugly Tuna *did* have a back entrance, not open to the public, that led out to an adjacent construction site. This back entrance happened to be the only means of exiting the bar that was not covered by a CCTV camera. But, if Brian had somehow snuck out of the bar in this manner without telling his friends, the obvious question would therefore be *why*? Assuming the theory that no foul play was involved, and Brian disappeared from both the bar and life as he knew it purely of his own free will, what could possibly have been his motivation?

Later details that came to light suggested that a *few* dark clouds may have existed in the ostensibly sunny skies of Brian's life. His mother, Rene, with whom he had been quite close, had died of cancer shortly before his disappearance. This loss had apparently affected Brian greatly, and some have speculated it could have fostered in him a hidden depression that may have played a role in his disappearance. But many who knew him assert that Brian's grief in losing his mother had played a major role in his desire to become a doctor in the first place, and much of his drive to finish medical school and begin a medical career was based on his desire to help others dealing with the same illnesses that took his mother's life. Would he then want to abandon it all in one brazen act of vanishing?

Later reports came to light that, on the night of his disappearance, Brian had, in fact, engaged in some kind of verbal altercation with one of his friends. The cause and severity of this argument are unclear, but some have speculated that *this* may have played some sort of role in Brian's disappearance. Columbus Police did reach out to the friend in question, requesting an interview and, potentially, a polygraph test. However, the friend refused the polygraph and eventually got in touch with an attorney rather than answering questions. Though some may see this as suspicious, police were unable to uncover any further evidence of foul play on the friend's part, and the investigation into him was eventually abandoned as a dead end. Even if one were to believe that this friend did commit some act of foul play against Brian, the question still remains how this person could have murdered him so discreetly so as to avoid detection from anyone else in the crowded bar, and then, even more bafflingly, dispose of the body so thoroughly that no trace of it has been found to this day?

Chapter 3
Jodi Huisentruit, Disappeared in 1995

The most tragic irony of the sinister 1995 disappearance of Jodi Huisentruit is how she could vanish—seemingly into thin air—after building a career of being one of the *most* visible residents of Mason City, Iowa. By June of 1995, the 27-year-old Huisentruit had earned a spot as a morning news anchor for KIMT, Mason City's local CBS affiliate. Thus, in the summer of 1995, Huisentruit's smiling face had become quite recognizable within the small Iowa city, acting as something of a pleasing, reassuring wake-up call for most Mason City residents, regardless of what news greeted them each morning. Huisentruit's disappearance, and the ominous details surrounding it, therefore became a particularly nasty gut-punch to the small town, which had up until then prided itself on its relatively safe "small town" values and friendly community.

As Huisentruit herself might have reported on her morning newscast, the facts are as follows. On June 27, 1995, just before dawn, Huisentruit failed to show up for her morning shift at KIMT's Mason City broadcasting station. Given her early schedule, Huisentruit usually needed to arrive at work around 4 AM. However, according to co-workers, she wasn't known to be the most punctual person to ever work the morning news shift, and occasional tardiness, coupled with profuse apologies and off-hand explanations, were not exactly uncommon with her. Thus, when 4 AM rolled around, and Huisentruit failed to show up, few people in the office assumed anything particularly sinister was afoot. Indeed, KIMT producer Amy Kuns was able to call Huisentruit's apartment directly. She managed to get hold of Huisentruit herself, who was apologetic at oversleeping and assuring the station that she would be arriving shortly. At this point, Huisentruit's failure to show up for work brought about little more than some low-key annoyance among her co-workers, and nobody at that hour assumed any of the further developments that continue to haunt Mason City to this day.

    Despite her assurances over the phone, 5 AM rolled around, and Huisentruit still had not shown up. Then, 6 AM. With the station's morning broadcast schedule pressing in on them, Kuns herself was eventually forced to fill in for Huisentruit on the station's morning programming. At this point, most of her co-workers still assumed that Huisentruit would appear at the station at any moment, profusely apologetic and sputtering some story about forgetting to set her alarm or some such thing. Undoubtedly the worst that would come from this would be some light ribbing from her co-workers and maybe an irritated lecture from the station's management. But by the time the morning program concluded around 7 AM, Huisentruit was still nowhere to be found. Now somewhat concerned, her co-workers once again tried calling her apartment. This time, however, no one answered. At this time, just before the widespread usage of cell phones, her KIMT co-workers had no clear means of getting in contact with the missing Huisentruit. Perhaps still trying to push their darker apprehensions out of mind, around 7 AM, the station, at last, made a call to the Mason City police, requesting that an officer be sent to her apartment for a welfare check.

    At the time, Huisentruit was living in the Key Apartments complex, only about a five-minute drive from the KIMT studio. When police first arrived there on the morning of June 27, things initially seemed encouraging. Huisentruit's red Mazda Miata was still parked in front of her building, and undoubtedly police assumed, when they buzzed her apartment, they would encounter Huisentruit herself, still groggy and somewhat perturbed at herself for having overslept so long. But attempts at reaching Huisentruit in her apartment turned up nothing, and police eventually determined that Huisentruit was no longer there. Turning their attention to her car, they began to uncover more disturbing pieces of evidence. A quick search turned up Huisentruit's car keys, lying on the ground next to the car, with one key bent as if caught in some kind of struggle. Turning their attention to Huisentruit's neighbours, police soon heard many around the apartment complex report having heard screams earlier that morning, around the time that Huisentruit would have been leaving for work (assuming that she had left her apartment shortly after her phone conversation with Kuns). However, no one saw the exact source of the screams, so no clear source or description of events could be determined. A few witnesses did report seeing an unfamiliar white van in the apartment complex's parking lot, near the vicinity of where Huisentruit's car was parked. However, no one was able to recall a license plate number or any other unique identifying features. As large, white vans were not exactly uncommon in the area, this did little to help with the investigation.

And those remain the known facts in their entirety, the totality of what would be reported by local news anchors like Huisentruit herself in their succinct and to-the-point morning news broadcasts. Despite a subsequent 25 years of searching, no sign of Huisentruit has ever been found. Of course, this has not been for lack of awareness in the Mason City area. Being such a public figure in the local media, Huisentruit's disappearance and potential abduction sent shockwaves through the small town. KIMT, the station that was initially annoyed at Huisentruit's failure to show up for work on time, quickly dedicated much of their broadcast scheduling to intensive coverage of the subsequent police investigation into Huisentruit's disappearance and any and all new evidence or leads that may come up. Her co-workers, both on-air and off, wore white ribbons in her honour, and across the town local businesses, volunteers, and community leaders dedicated their time and resources to try and bring Huisentruit home. But these efforts ultimately turned up nothing, and after years of no breaks in the case, Huisentruit's family finally made the difficult decision to have her declared legally dead in May of 2001.

As for where the investigation stands today, thus far, only two specific suspects have ever been identified in any serious capacity. The first suspect, the earliest one to come to investigators' attention, was John Vansice. Vansice was a friend of Huisentruit, despite being a good deal older than her, who had been with her the night before her disappearance. As Huisentruit has recently turned 27, Vansice had been with her during her recent birthday celebration, and on the night before June 27 had apparently invited Huisentruit over to his house to show her a videotape of the celebration that he had compiled. Being the last known person to see Huisentruit alive and lacking any other clear leads, Vansice initially became the police's main suspect. But Vansice was able to pass a polygraph test administered by detectives, and lacking any other evidence, the investigation into Vansice ultimately became a dead end.

     A second, potentially more promising lead would find its way to the police a few years later. A Minnesota jailhouse informant informed police that a cellmate of his, a former college basketball player named Tony Jackson, then serving a life sentence for a series of sexual assaults, had bragged in prison about abducting and murdering a TV news anchorwoman. Further investigations into Jackson revealed that he appeared to have an interest in news broadcasting and TV journalism, and had once had a girlfriend who bore a resemblance to Huisentruit. However, though this lead was pursued (including searches and the use of cadaver dogs on areas indicated by the information given about Jackson), no further evidence incriminating Jackson in Huisentruit's disappearance ever came to light.

Chapter 4
Ben Needham, Disappeared in 1991

As was the case with Amy Lynn Bradley, the disappearance of Ben Needham in 1991 has since prompted a surge in potential sightings, blurring the line between which leads are credible and which are not. But unlike the Bradley case, Needham's disappearance was further complicated by the fact that he was not even two years old when he vanished, forcing investigators to rely on artificial aging technology and follow leads of any younger boy who meets Needham's vague description of a blonde-haired toddler. Thus, though sighting after sighting is reported virtually every year, Needham's mother is still no closer to determining what happened to her young son than she was on the day he vanished.

Ben Needham was born in 1989 in the British town of Boston, Lincolnshire, to a young single mother named Kerry Needham. In July of 1991, Kerry and 21-month-old Ben moved to the Greek island of Kos in the South-eastern Aegean Sea to live with Kerry's parents, who at the time were renovating a house on the island. Kerry took a job at a nearby hotel to support the family during the summer, going to work during the day and leaving her toddler son in the care of her parents while they worked on the house. Here, young Ben would often be seen playing around the property, wandering in and out of construction sites and occasionally getting a ride on his uncle's moped. Then, on July 24, 1991, while his mother was at work, Ben vanished somewhere on the property, never to be seen again.

Many of the issues surrounding the case have been blamed on the local Greek police. Upon first receiving the report of the missing boy, the Greek Hellenistic Police force initially honed in on the Needhams themselves as suspects. This, undoubtedly, made sense from an investigatory perspective, but the police also neglected other paths of inquiry early on in the investigation, including the theory that Ben had been abducted by someone outside of the family. Because of this single focus on the part of the police, the docks and airports on the relatively small island were not notified of the missing boy or his appearance until much later, giving potential abductors a large window of time to escape the island itself. Many have also charged that the Greek police lacked the resources or experience to adequately investigate disappearances like this and may have been in over their heads in the initial (and most crucial) stage of the investigation. Unsurprisingly, this initial investigation turned up nothing. After eleven days, Nikolaos Dakouras, the Kos chief of police, was quoted as saying: "We now believe we have searched every possible part of that area, and the boy is not there. It leaves us with a great mystery. We have no theories. We have no solutions." Also, unsurprisingly, police from the Needham family's native U.K. eventually got involved in the case.

With the abduction theory soon taking hold as the story gained steam across the U.K. and Europe, sightings of the young boy began to pour into police hotlines. Many of these reports, unfortunately, fell more in line with pre-existing cultural prejudices than any potentially useful information. In particular, a large number of Ben Needham "sightings" involved the observation of suspiciously-blonde children among dark-haired Romani people (also known derogatively as "Gypsies"). Romani, a historically persecuted and ostracized group in Europe, often found themselves the subject of police interrogations prompted by the appearance of any light-haired child found in their care, even if subsequent DNA testing and records searches demonstrated that these children were not, in fact, Ben Needham. As the years went by, Needham, if he were still alive, would have grown beyond the chubby-faced toddler that he was in the pictures displayed across the news. Sightings thus became less and less reliable, with any blonde-haired young boy in Greece becoming a potential lead. Despite extensive searches by the Greek and British police *and* the Greek Army, and a renewed effort in 1993 following a formal request by then-

U.K. Prime Minister John Major, the case eventually went cold, with no trace of the young boy ever being uncovered.

In 2016, a new and potentially promising theory came to light. South Yorkshire Police, who had been overseeing the case from the British side, received a tip of a recently-deceased Greek construction worker from Kos, who had apparently made the death bed confession that he had accidentally killed the young boy with his excavator while working on the Needham family house, and had buried the body on sight in a panic. In seeking to pursue this lead to the fullest, police launched one of the most intricate and extensive searches yet, targeting a particular mounded area near the Needham's former Kos home with teams of forensic investigators and cadaver dogs. At first, this search appeared to turn up some promising findings. Police uncovered a small toy car *and* a young child's sandal from the scene, two items that investigators believed may have belonged to Needham. Even more promising, forensic testing on the toy and the sandal revealed traces of human DNA, potentially from blood, which gave police a more solid means of connecting the items to Needham. However, after extensive testing, the South Yorkshire police finally announced in 2018 that the DNA found on these items was *not* a match to the Needham family. Despite their initial promise, both of these potential clues ended up as dead ends, and no further traces of Ben were uncovered in the extensive search.

Thus, as of now, the disappearance of young Ben Needham remains a mystery. If Needham is, in fact, still alive, he would be in his early 30s as of this writing and would likely have no clear memory of a potential abduction or similar from among his earliest childhood experiences. However, while recent forensic testing on both the toy car and the sandal did not provide a DNA match to Ben, police now regard the "accidental death" theory as the most credible. Jon Cousins, a Detective Inspector with the South Yorkshire Police who had led the recently-renewed investigation, stated: that the young boy had most likely died as a result of an "accident," probably close by the farmhouse where he was last seen. Still, without a body and without a direct confession, the case remains open. Kerry Needham to this day still holds out hope, if not to be reunited with her still-living son, at least to receive some degree of closure and knowledge of what happened to him that day in 1991.

Chapter 5
Renata Antczak, Disappeared in 2017

Though the most recent case to appear on our list, the 2017 disappearance of 49-year-old Renata Antczak, has nonetheless captivated a nation and brought forth scores of theories. Antczak, a native of Poland, was living in the British city of Hull with her husband and two young daughters. On the morning of April 25, 2017, Antczak was seen dropping her younger daughter off at Broadacre Primary School in Hull. She apparently wore a distinctive yellow jacket as she pulled away from the school, off to do whatever maternal chores would likely consume her day. At least, that was most likely the thought of the other parents who engage in friendly chatting with their fellows during the daily routine of school drop-offs. At the time, none of them would have likely thought that they would be the last known people to see Antczak alive. But later that night, after failing to come home, her husband contacted police to report her missing. What followed was one of the largest investigations in the history of the small Yorkshire city. One that, despite countless resources, man hours, and media appeals, has so far turned up no answers.

In the subsequent years after her disappearance, the search has extended beyond the city of Hull itself into much of the rest of the country, as well as into Antczak's native Poland. But, as of this writing, police have uncovered no leads, evidence, or trace of the missing woman. Police have actually admitted as much, with Detective Superintendent Tony Cockerill stating that they had exhausted all of their lines of inquiry, which had proven to be "fruitless," and that he could think of no other person "on Earth" who may know where Antczak may be.

However, police *do* believe that foul play was involved in Antczak's disappearance, with Cockerill stating that he still believed that case to be in the realm of a homicide investigation. But the questions of who murdered Antczak, for what motive, and where her remains may be found remain unanswered.

The most obvious suspect, as in most cases of this nature, would, of course, be Antczak's husband. And, following a deeper investigation, the issue of Antczak's marriage initially appeared to potentially bear fruit in terms of answers as to what happened to her. Antczak's husband, a dentist named Majid Mustafa, has thus far maintained his innocence in the case. But, though she has since come to be defined by her final image as a happy, dedicated mother lovingly dropping her child off at school, a deeper search reveals that not all was right in her domestic life. According to friends, she and Mustafa's marriage had become increasingly troubled, with the couple apparently fighting more and more frequently. According to certain credible reports, Antczak had even told friends that she was considering filing for divorce.

But even darker information would soon come out after Antczak's disappearance. Shortly after his wife went missing, Mustafa himself was arrested on the charge of attempting to attain Gamma Hydroxybutyrate, or GHB, a well-known date rape drug that he was apparently planning to use on Antczak herself. According to reports, Mustafa suspected at the time that Antczak was having an affair and appeared to have contacted a friend to procure the sedative for the purpose of drugging her and subsequently unlocking her phone in an attempt to search for any evidence of infidelity. According to the criminal complaint, Mustafa was also planning on planting surveillance devices on Antczak's car out of a paranoid drive to root out suspected unfaithfulness on his wife's part. In 2018, Mustafa was sentenced to one year of conditional discharge for the offense, but as of 2021, no criminal charges have yet been brought against him in relation to his wife's actual disappearance.

Though Mustafa remains the prime suspect in most circles—for obvious reasons—no clear evidence has come to light specifically implicating him in Antczak's disappearance. Mustafa, of course, maintains his complete innocence to this day, and with no trace of Antczak yet to be found, nor any other clues that could lead to a break in the case, the question of what happened to Renata Antczak after she dropped her daughter off at school remains, as of now, a mystery.

Chapter 6
Rebecca Coriam, Disappeared in 2011

Finally, we end our section on disappearances where we began: at sea. More specifically, we come back to another mysterious disappearance on a cruise ship, perhaps highlighting the potentially dark underbelly of the family fun that cruise lines seek to portray out into the world. And, like the Amy Lynn Bradley case, the disappearance of Rebecca Coriam has the same strange details, the same lack of clear evidence, and the same shady and secretive behaviour from a company that advertises itself as a steward of peace and relaxation at sea.

In 2011, Rebecca Coriam was a crew member on the cruise ship *Disney Wonder*. *Disney Wonder* was part of the massive fleet of Disney Cruise Lines, the maritime division of the vast Disney corporate empire. Coriam herself was a 24-year-old native of the British city of Chester. After graduating from Plymouth University and serving for a time as a volunteer with the British Army cadets, Coriam applied for and secured a position with Disney cruise lines, eventually being assigned as a youth counsellor on the *Disney Wonder* during its voyages off the Pacific Coast of California and Mexico. A few months before her disappearance, Coriam took a brief leave of absence from work to return to Chester following her grandfather's death. This would, as it turned out, be the last time her family saw her in person.

On the morning of March 21, 2011, the *Disney Wonder* departed from Los Angeles for its scheduled voyage to the Mexican resort towns of Cabo San Lucas and Puerto Vallarta. Coriam had, up to this point, kept in contact with her family via Facebook and Skype. Indeed, on the morning of the 21st, she had even sent her parents a Facebook message, telling them that she would call the following day after her shift ended. Shortly thereafter, Coriam was captured on the ship's CCTV cameras in the crew lounge. The video shows Coriam speaking on her mobile phone, apparently distraught over the conversation. Though the video has no audio affixed, a fellow passenger can be seen coming up to her, apparently asking her if everything is okay. Coriam can then be seen saying what appears to be "yeah, fine," after which she leaves the lounge. This would be the last trace of Coriam to be uncovered thus far.

A few hours later, at around 9 AM pacific time, Coriam was scheduled to begin her daily shift as a ship youth worker. When she failed to report, her crewmates embarked on a search of the crew lounges, her room, and other common areas of the ship, finding no trace of her. After she failed to turn up in response to an announcement on the ship's public address system, her co-workers began to go from annoyed to concerned. However, as was the case with Amy Lynn Bradley, the official response from the ship's management was seemingly to prioritize the "festive" atmosphere among the ship's passengers over the well-being of their missing employee, or the need to embark on a much more comprehensive investigation shortly after her disappearance. Meanwhile, back in the U.K. Coriam's mother began to grow concerned when her daughter did not call them as she had earlier promised she would.

Though an investigation into Coriam's disappearance was launched soon after she had vanished—at an ostensibly quicker pace than the delayed investigation following the disappearance of Amy Lynn Bradley—the investigation itself was marred by errors, oversights, and overlapping jurisdictions that rendered the possibility of a quick solution less and less possible. One major complication was that the ship itself, though owned by an American company, was registered in the Bahamas. This is, in fact, a common practice among the cruise ship industry, especially among ships operating in and around the Caribbean and Pacific Coast of North America. As the ship was in international waters when Coriam disappeared, the Royal Bahamas Police Force had jurisdiction over the investigation onboard the ship itself. However, though a Bahamian detective did fly to the ship to investigate the disappearance, he did not make it there until the ship had returned to Los Angeles several days later. What's more, the detective later admitted to Coriam's parents that he had only spent one day on board the ship and had only interviewed a relatively small number of crew members (and no passengers) before returning to the Bahamas. Additionally, the search for Coriam's body at sea was likely marred by further legal and jurisdictional difficulties. The relatively large section of international waters where Coriam may have fallen overboard fell under the legal authority of both the United States Coast Guard *and* the Mexican Navy. Both launched extensive searches, but cooperation proved difficult to achieve given the complexities of such a search from both a legal and logistical perspective. Thus, despite an extensive search from both American and Mexican authorities, no trace of Coriam was found at sea.

In the decade since her disappearance, Coriam's family and friends have directed much of their ire at Disney itself, as well as the investigative bodies who failed to locate any trace of their daughter. As with the Bradley disappearance, Coriam's parents have charged that Disney was far more concerned with protecting itself from legal liability than they were in locating their daughter. According to reports, when Coriam's parents were flown to Los Angeles following their daughter's disappearance, Disney had them transported to the ship in a nondescript SUV with blackened-out windows and only allowed them to enter the ship itself through a side employee entrance, *after* the ship's passengers had left. What's more, Coriam's parents have since asserted that Disney has been less than forthcoming with relevant information as to their daughter's disappearance, communicating mainly through attorneys and vague written statements and sharing little in the way of relevant information.

Criticism of the investigation has also come from the British government. In 2011, Stephen Mosley, a member of the House of Commons representing Coriam's constituency, openly criticized the investigation and Disney's response, calling it "appalling" and advocating for new laws that would allow British authorities to investigate the deaths and disappearances of British citizens on maritime vessels, even those registered under the flags of other countries.

In November of 2011, journalist Jon Ronson published a lengthy investigation of Coriam's disappearance in *The Guardian* newspaper. In conducting his own investigation, Ronson booked himself passage on the *Disney Wonder* itself, going on the same voyage that Coriam was working at the time of her disappearance. According to his account, he was able to hear underhand accounts from Coriam's crewmates, hinting that more information of her disappearance existed but was being actively suppressed by Disney. According to these accounts, many of Coriam's co-workers aboard the ship believed that she had, in fact, fallen overboard while relaxing at the crew pool on the ship's Deck #5, just before the start of her shift. In these accounts, the ship was struck with inclement weather, which created enough of a list in the ship's orientation to cause Coriam to slip off the side of the boat and fall into the ocean. However, Ronson himself came to doubt this theory after examining the crew pool itself. He noted that the walls surrounding the pool were quite high and reinforced with safety apparatuses, making it highly unlikely that someone could be swept overboard from the area, even in extremely rough weather. Still, Ronson reports that most of the crew members he spoke to swear by this theory. Many also noted to him that Disney has in its possession specific information confirming the account, which they are actively covering up.

Ronson himself developed the theory that Coriam, rather than falling from the #5 deck's staff pool, actually fell from the #4 deck's jogging track. Coriam was known to be an avid jogger who would often spend her spare time taking laps on the ship's jogging track between shifts. Plus, Ronson noted that the walls alongside the jogging track were much shorter and less fortified than the walls around the staff pool, making it more likely that someone could accidentally fall overboard from there in any kind of inclement weather.

However, when pressing the ship's crew, Ronson got an unusual answer, one that had not apparently been released to either the press or Coriam's family—apparently several crew members had actually witnessed Coriam falling overboard from the #5 deck pool. What's more, crew members confided in Ronson that Disney, in fact, *had* the security footage of Coriam's fall but was actively covering it up to avoid legal jeopardy. The pool theory *was* seemingly supported when it came to light that the crew had found female flip-flops at the pool shortly after Coriam went missing. However, Coriam's family denied that these had belonged to her (in addition to not being her style, they apparently were not even the correct size), and later on, they were identified as belonging to a different crew member entirely.

If Coriam did fall from the crew pool on the #5 deck, as her co-workers seem to believe happened, the height of the surrounding walls and the existence of additional safety precautions would make it more likely that Coriam *jumped* rather than fell in some kind of tragic accident. Based on the last-known security footage of her, Coriam had appeared emotionally distraught following a phone conversation, and some friends did report that Coriam may have been more depressed than her family believed (though these accounts have not been verified). Still, there are also several signs that Coriam herself was planning on living beyond the day of her disappearance—for example, she had apparently purchased tickets to Disneyland for herself and her family to surprise them with following the end of the ship's voyage. Thus, if Coriam *did* commit suicide, the act would have been highly impulsive. This is not necessarily uncommon in suicide cases, but the lack of clear evidence one way or the other does make the case all that more frustrating.

One point, though, that does seem to be consistent among the different theories and explanations is that Disney knows more about the case than they are letting on. To this date, Disney refused to officially release the number and locations of all of the CCTV cameras onboard the *Disney Wonder*. Indeed, many of them are hidden and out of view of the general passengers. However, during his investigation, Ronson did note several in view when he toured both the #4 deck jogging track and the #5 deck crew pool. This means that, had Coriam fallen (or jumped) overboard at either location—or on most other potential locations on the ship—it would most likely have been captured on the ship's security footage. If Disney *were* suppressing evidence of Coriam's death, it would be quite in line with how her parents have spoken of their treatment by Disney executives during the course of the investigation—while outwardly sympathetic and helpful, in actuality highly obfuscating and surreptitious, as if they have something to hide.

So, did Rebecca Coriam fall overboard the *Disney Wonder* in a tragic accident? Did she jump? Or did something more sinister occur? Was she murdered by a fellow crewmate? Or did she maybe fall victim to the alleged fate of Amy Lynn Bradley and end up abducted by human traffickers? Whatever the ultimate explanation for her disappearance is, the answer might lie somewhere, buried deep in the Disney vault. But until Disney's conscience overrides their desire to protect their happy, family-friendly "brand," the rest of the world may never know the answer.

Chapter 7
The Incident at Dyatlov Pass

Given the decades of Cold War intrigue, conspiracies, and sinister mysteries that have incubated in the secrecy behind the Iron Curtain, the fact that the Dyatlov Pass Incident is considered by many to be the most mysterious unsolved case arising from the former Soviet Union should give most casual observers a good idea of how bizarre this case is. On a surface level, the deaths of nine hikers in the remote and unforgiving wilderness of the Ural Mountains (in a Russian winter, no less) should not raise too many questions. A tragedy, no doubt, but such tragedies are not exactly unheard of among those few daring souls who test their mettle by brazing such harsh landscapes. But when one looks a bit closer into the case itself and the details brought to light in the subsequent investigation, the unexplained details, bizarre findings, and downright ominous pieces of evidence begin to compound, turning the Dyatlov Pass Incident from a standard expeditionary tragedy to something else entirely. In the 60+ years since the tragedy befell that group of nine hikers, theories have ranged from Soviet military tests to UFOs, all the way to Yetis and interdimensional beings. But, while theories can come and go, the truth of what happened likely died alongside those nine hikers on that frozen mountainous landscape.

In the cold January of 1959, ten experienced Soviet hikers set off on a multi-day hiking and skiing expedition across the Ural Mountains in the Sverdlovsk Oblast, then part of the Russian Soviet Socialist Republic. The group—eight men and two women—mainly consisted of younger students from the nearby Ural Polytechnical Institute. The group's leader was 23-year-old Igor Dyatlov, a radio engineering student who, unbeknownst to anyone at the time, would posthumously lend his name to the mountainous region where he and his friends would soon meet their violent deaths. Accompanying Dyatlov on the trip were Yuri Doroshenko (age 21), Lyudmila Dubinina (age 20), Georgiy Krivonischenko (age 23), Alexander Kolevatov (age 24), Zinaida Kolmogorova (age 22), Rustem Slobodin (age 23), Nikolai Thibeaux-Brignolles (age 23), Semyon Zolotaryov (age 38), and Yuri Yudin (age 21). Based on contemporary reports, the expedition was approved by the local Physical Culture and Sport Commission for the general purpose of the hikers achieving greater certification as hikers and outdoorsmen. At the time, all ten expedition members had level II hiker certification, the second-highest level of expertise. In order to achieve level III (the highest level), the hikers would need to log 300 kilometres of hiking experience, which the group could achieve by completing their winter trek across the Ural Mountains and returning without incident. The group's itinerary, as it was approved by the commission, would have taken them through the Northern Ural Mountains, across the Lozva River, and eventually to the remote Otorten Mountain.

If the group had looked closely at this itinerary during their planning stage, they might have noticed that the route would also take them past a seemingly unassuming and indistinct mountain listed as "Kholat Syakhl." Of course, unless any of the hikers could speak the language of the region's indigenous Mansi people, they may not have realized that this name translated to "Dead Mountain." Or, even if they did, the notion that this may have been an ominous omen was lost in the surrounding enthusiasm and excitement.

The trip was not expected to be an easy one. In addition to the rough and remote mountainous terrain, winter temperatures in the Ural Mountains can fall to around as low as -30 degrees Celsius. Still, the difficulty of the trek would have been well-known to the experienced group and would, after all, help them in achieving their highest certification as hikers. Thus, on January 23, 1959, the group of ten set off from Sverdlovsk City (today the city of Yekaterinburg, Russia), taking a train to the smaller mountainous town of Ivdel. On January 25, they took a bus to the even smaller village of Vizhai, essentially a truck stop that served as the last bit of civilization they would encounter before immersing themselves in the pure mountain wilderness. According to reports from locals, the group seemed to be in jovial spirits that night, purchasing a hearty meal and several loaves of bread in order to pack on as many calories as they could before embarking on foot for the true start of their tough journey the following day.

These reports, as they have later come out, paint a happy picture of the group. One likes to imagine them engaging in friendly banter, perhaps imbibing in one last round of vodka before immersing themselves in the rugged Ural wilderness, perhaps joking and chattering with excitement at the prospect of completing their most challenging expedition to date and ultimately joining the ranks of the Soviet Union's most elite outdoorsmen. If any among the group felt an inkling of foreboding that this journey would not result in the successful triumph that they were boasting of, but rather something much worse, he or she did not let it out in the otherwise festive atmosphere.

On the morning of January 27, the group finally departed on foot from Vizhai and entered the wilderness proper. Within a day, however, the expedition hit its first snag. 21-year-old Yuri Yudin found himself stricken with a sudden health issue that forced him to abandon the expedition and turn back to civilization. Though an experienced hiker, Yudin did apparently suffer from a few chronic health issues, including rheumatism and sciatica. On the morning of January 28, Yudin determined that the sudden downturn in his health made his continuation on the expedition much more dangerous, and his continued presence would put into jeopardy the chances of the entire group completing their journey. So, Yudin, no doubt disappointed and apologetic, said goodbye to his friends and reluctantly made the trip back to civilization. One here might wish to stop and imagine Yudin's mindset at this moment. Perhaps he was angry at the hand the fates had dealt him. Perhaps he was somewhat embarrassed for showing himself to be "weaker" than his friends, who would have the opportunity to complete such an exciting trip without him. Little could he know just how lucky he would prove to be in only a few days or how this stroke of what initially appeared to be misfortune would soon prove to be anything but. Ironically, though he was forced to abandon the expedition early, Yudin later became a crucial source of information for possible explanations of the group's subsequent actions.

Though undoubtedly sad at the loss of their friend, the remaining nine members of the expedition nonetheless judiciously continued on their planned route that same day. At this point, we who are looking back on the case can only speculate as to what the remaining nine were thinking over the next few days. But, pictures later recovered show the group seemingly happy, often posing in friendly and jovial group shots, smiling and making faces at the camera. For the next few days, despite the rough terrain and deathly cold of the landscape, the Dyatlov group did not appear to be in over their heads or show any signs of foreboding of potential dangers that they may face.

From this point on, the exact timeline of their remaining journey can only be guessed at, going by the clues later uncovered in the subsequent investigation sometime after the fact. Most experts on the case believe that the group made it to the edge of the flatter lowland forest areas by January 31 and began to prepare for the subsequent climb over the next few days through the steeper, more mountainous terrain. It was at this point that the group would likely have come into the proximity of the now-infamous Kholat Syakhl, or "Dead Mountain." Though they wouldn't have known it, it was also here that the group began to move through the mountainous pass that now bears the name of the leader of their ill-fated expedition, Igor Dyatlov.

Based on what investigators later found and what the former expedition member Yudin later speculated, we can adhere to the following timeline for what happened between February 1 and 2. As the group approached Kholat Syakhl through their eponymous Dyatlov Pass, the weather probably took a turn against them, with heavy, gale-force winds beginning to pour down from the mountain and thick snowdrifts potentially obscuring their vision. In these worsening conditions, the group may have gotten turned around somewhat, taking a wrong turn westward and going farther up the slope of Kholat Syakhl than they had intended. Yudin later speculated that, upon realizing the error, Dyatlov decided to pitch camp there rather than turn back the way that they came, as he may not have wanted to lose too much of the altitude that they had gained. Whatever the cause, on the night of February 1 or 2, the group set up camp higher up on the side of Kholat Syakhl, above the treeline, and about a kilometre away from the thicker forest behind them that would have provided a bit more shelter from the winter conditions. And this, as it so happens, is the last fact that is known definitively about the expedition. Whatever happened next has, for the past 60 years, existed purely in the realm of speculation, theory, and conspiracy.

Before departing, Dyatlov had informed their sponsoring athletic club that the group would send them a telegram when they had completed their circular trek around Otorten Mountain and returned to Vizhai. Based upon their tentative timeline, Dyatlov had predicted that the telegram would arrive around February 12, though given the number of variables that could affect the length of their trek, this timeframe could, of course, vary somewhat. Thus, when February 12 came and went, and no telegram from the group arrived, the Sverdlovsk Physical Culture and Sports Committee did not think too much of it. But then another day went by. And then another. And still, no word from the group made its way back to the sports committee or to the university. Beginning to feel a degree of concern, the organizing committee reached out to the few residents of Vizhai to see if *they* had seen any trace of the group. But the answer, of course, was *no*.

By February 20, the group had not been seen for nearly a month, with more than seven days elapsing since

Dyatlov's conservative estimate as to when they would return to civilization. At this point, even sudden variables such as inclement weather or an injury should not have prevented *anyone* in the group from making it back to Vizhai to telegram Sverdlovsk.

Unless, of course, something far worse had happened.

However, despite mounting concerns on the part of the committee itself, it turned out to be the family and friends of the missing hikers who finally managed to spur official action. On the 20th of February, 1959, a little less than a month since the group was last seen, the Ural Polytechnical Institute and Sverdlovsk Physical Culture and Sports Committee, at last, organized the first search party. This party, alas, would not quite be up to the heavy task, consisting primarily of volunteers and drawing mostly from the university's students and faculty. The local police and Soviet military did not get involved in the search until a few days later, providing much-needed supplies and logistical support. Still, given that the area in which the expedition had gone missing was quite large and that the weather was still inclement, it wouldn't be another several more days that the first traces of the group would be discovered.

As it happened, the expedition's campsite on the slope of Kholat Syakhl was discovered not by the military or police but by another university student named Mikhail Sharavin. By February 26, the date that the remains of the camp were found, it is likely that the rescue team had already braced themselves for the worst. Certainly, most would have tried to hold out some hope that the group had managed to survive somehow for all that time in the harsh Ural wilderness, but the length at which they had been missing and the brutality of the winter weather made that scenario less and less likely as the days went on. Still, though the discovery of the dead bodies of several expedition members would have been a grim but not necessarily surprising development in the search, the particular scene the Sharavin uncovered on the slopes of Kholat Syakhl on February 26 was more horrifying than they had allowed themselves to fear. It also immediately presented a mystery of something far more sinister, yet also more mysterious, than a simple camping mishap.

The condition of the tent and the few bodies discovered by the search party of February 26 has since fallen into legend, sparking wave after wave of conflicting theories and attempts at explanation. But first, let's examine just what exactly Sharavin and the rest of the search party discovered on the side of the mountain. The first thing that they found was the group's tent. Most ominously, and mysteriously, was the condition that it was in. While rough winds and exposure would have left some wear and tear, the tent, as it was found, had undergone much more severe damage. The tent was buried under a deep layer of snow and had been torn down and cut into pieces, almost appearing as half a bundle of rags rather than a functioning tent. A closer investigation of the tent uncovered two more disturbing facts. First, the search party quickly discovered, to their likely horror, that, while none of the expedition members themselves were inside, their clothing, gear, and belongings *were*. This meant that the actual expedition members had gone out of their tent, into the deadly cold and brutal elements, *without proper clothing or equipment*. Secondly, and perhaps even more disturbingly, was the fact that the tent appeared to have been deliberately torn apart by human hands. But, upon further investigation, the search party noticed something else, something that raised even more questions: the tent appeared to have been cut apart *from the inside*. Thus, even before locating any bodies, the search party was suddenly faced with a bizarre and sinister scenario, one which continues to puzzle investigators and theorists to this day. The group, bundled up in the relative safety of their tent, had suddenly fled with such urgency that they felt the need to not only *cut* themselves out but then *flee* into -30 degree temperatures in only their sleeping clothes.

Though several weeks had passed since whatever incident had transpired, the team was able to find footprints of the expedition members leading away from the ruined tent. These prints, however, only added to the mystery. The prints seemed to show that the hikers had fled from the tent either completely barefoot or wearing inadequate footwear. This, of course, did not bode particularly well. In temperatures as cold as the Ural winter nights, frostbite can occur within minutes, and most could have guessed that not even the hardiest hiker would survive long with such little clothing in these kinds of elements. But, though fearing the worst, the search party followed the prints as best they could, down the slope of the mountain and into a thicket of trees farther down.

Entering the forest, the party made a grim but not (at that point) unexpected discovery. Two of the hikers' bodies were lying around a pine tree, close to what looked like an attempt at a campfire. These two bodies were later determined to be those of Krivonischenko and Doroshenko. A closer examination of the scene revealed something else interesting. The pine tree around which the two bodies had been grouped bore signs of damage as if someone had attempted to climb it. Upon looking closer, searchers did, in fact, discover bits of clothing attached to some of the tree's higher branches, confirming the theory that at least one of the hikers had attempted to climb the tree, perhaps trying to locate the ruined tent to find his or her way back. Circling around, the searchers eventually uncovered three more bodies in the space between the pine tree and the camp—those of Slobodin, Kolmogorova, and Dyatlov himself.

By this point, everyone in the search party recognized that something catastrophic had occurred, and no realistic hope existed that the remaining four hikers, still unaccounted for among the bodies, could still be alive somewhere. But even as the five found bodies were transported back to the proper authorities for further investigation, the search party, in addition to their general grief at the loss of life, was also left with a deep sense of confusion and unease and the details they had uncovered.

Dyatlov's group had all been experienced hikers and mountaineers. Having dealt with brutal Russian winters first-hand, no one in the group would have been under any false impressions of the real mortal threat posed by the extreme cold and deadly conditions that would have waited for them outside of their tent that night. So, *why* then did they not only flee into unsurvivable temperatures but do so without even properly dressing themselves and, in fact, *cutting their own tent* from the inside?

One theory that was initially floated was that the party was struck by an avalanche. True, a sudden avalanche could pose enough of an immediate threat that the hikers would find themselves forced to flee into the "lesser" danger of the cold forest. But a quick examination of the remains of the campsite brought forth more questions than answers. Many members of the search party were likewise experienced outdoorsmen, some with military experience, and all possessing intimate familiarity with mountainous terrain in the wintertime. Based upon their experience, the campsite itself, though in disarray, did not show any recognizable signs of being hit with an avalanche in the past few weeks.

Standing on the side of the "Dead Mountain," watching the bodies of their fellow students and would-be mountaineers be carried away, looking at that ruined campsite and passing only silence back and forth between each other, did the members of the search party feel a sudden chill unrelated to the cold mountainous air surrounding them? Did they, even standing there in the apparent safety of daylight, begin anxiously glancing past their shoulders, subtly scanning the dense treeline or the whitened and mysterious slopes of the mountain that ascended above them?

As this initial discovery set off a chain reaction of more and more questions, the investigation into what might have happened forked into two distinct paths. The five bodies that had been recovered first were sent to a coroner's office to be examined, while, back on the mountain, search parties continued to parse the area for the bodies of the four remaining hikers—those of Thibeaux-Brignolles, Dubinina, Kolevatov, and Zolotaryov.

Despite their best efforts, more than two months passed before the remaining four bodies were found. On May 4, the remains of Thibeaux-Brignolles, Dubinina, Kolevatov, and Zolotaryov were finally located in a ravine about 70 meters away from the pine tree where the first two bodies had been discovered. The bodies were found buried under about four feet of snow. Upon an initial examination, all four appeared to be more heavily dressed than the other five, in some cases appearing to wear clothing taken from the other bodies closer towards the campsite. Even more strangely—and more ominously—despite the two months of decomposition, the four bodies found in the ravine had clearly suffered varying degrees of significant injuries. It seemed as if they had suffered several broken bones, including broken ribs and fractured skulls. More disturbingly, several of them were missing parts of their faces. Dubinina's body, for example, was found to be missing its tongue and lips, while Zolotaryov's body was missing its eyes.

Elsewhere, the other prong of the investigation was taking its course in a Soviet medical examiner's office. Shortly after their discovery, an autopsy on the first five bodies had concluded, unsurprisingly, that the cause of death in all five cases was hypothermia, or freezing to death. Given that the temperatures that night would have been well below zero and that no one in the group was wearing anywhere near sufficient clothing, this finding, at least, did not spark any further questions. However, the autopsies on these bodies *did* bring about a few lingering uncertainties. Though hypothermia was listed as the cause of death in all five cases, the autopsies did show additional injuries to the bodies.

At this point, the relative secrecy of the Soviet Union, the lack of comprehensive record-keeping, and the general information entropy that occurs over such a timespan make it somewhat difficult to get a complete picture of what sorts of injuries were found on these five bodies. At the very least, reports suggest that the medical examiners did find several cuts and bruises, injuries that would not necessarily be out of place should one suddenly be forced to flee a tent into the forest while wearing insufficient clothing. Yet, some reports, though difficult to confirm today, may suggest a darker truth. According to these reports, some of the bodies found near the pine tree had, in addition to standard cuts and bruises, several clear *burns*. A few reports even suggested that one body had missing chunks of flesh from its extremities that were later found *in its mouth*.

Of course, though, it was the eventual autopsies on the four bodies found in the ravine two months later that would reveal some of the most infamous details of the entire case. Unlike the first five bodies, the injuries found on these bodies were both more severe and more significant. Specifically, three of the four hikers found in the ravine were found to have *not* died of hypothermia. According to official medical examiner's reports, Dubinina and Zolotaryov both died of "severe chest trauma," trauma that had caused numerous broken ribs and likely internal bleeding. Thibeaux-Brignolles, on the other hand, was found to have a severe skull injury, one that would have been significant enough to potentially push fragments of skull into his brain. These injuries, of course, came in addition to the obvious loss of eyes and tongues on some of the bodies. However, arguably the most significant and mysterious detail, the one that has prompted the most speculation and confusion in the subsequent decades, was that these four bodies (despite burial under a thick layer of snow for two months in proximity to the running water of an underground stream) were found to possess "unnatural" levels of *radiation*.

And here is where the official Soviet investigation came to an end, at least as far as we can tell today. With so many strange details adding up—the bizarre flight from the tent into freezing temperatures, the injuries sustained by the bodies, the presence of radiation, etc.—the investigation quickly spiralled beyond normal capabilities. Though the case had initially seemed to be nothing more than a tragic—but explicable—case of overconfident hikers falling victim to the infamous Russian winter, investigators soon found themselves having to explain more and more bizarre details. Lacking sufficient answers to any of these questions and undoubtedly feeling increasing pressure from Soviet authorities, the investigators were ultimately forced to close the case with no clear explanation. In seeking to articulate their understanding of the case as best they could, the investigative body eventually released an official conclusion that has since become somewhat infamous in its vague but sinister phrasing: the nine hikers had died as a result of a "compelling natural force."

This explanation, unsurprisingly, has not exactly proven to be satisfactory to the countless people who have taken an interest in the case over the years. Thus, in the resulting void where a clear explanation would be, a number of different theories have taken root in the subsequent 60 years. These theories range from explicable natural phenomena to governmental coverups to things not of this world. Without clear records from the former Soviet Union, specific details may be somewhat hard to verify, making more imaginative speculation all the more tempting.

In terms of a "rational" explanation for the incident, the biggest challenge has been the compounding number of strange details that pop up the more one looks into the case. One *might* be able to explain the sudden flight from the tent in the dead of night well enough. One might even be able to explain most of the injuries found on the bodies. But to explain the flight from the tent, *and* the injuries, *and* the lack of clothing, *and* the missing tissue, *and* the placement of the bodies, *and* the reports of radiation contamination, all in one coherent and satisfactory explanation, begins to push the boundaries of credulity.

But, this does not mean that many experts have not tried. Thus, we will first look into the most comprehensive "rational" explanation provided by credible authorities today. This theory might more accurately be described as a sort of overlapping range of different theories, all derived from one or two specific elements of the case, and all concocted independently and moulded together in a kind of uneasy scaffolding of a theory.

The first question that must be answered is, of course, what caused the hikers to suddenly flee from their tent in the first place? And not only flee, but flee in such a panic that they needed to cut exit holes into their tents and flee into the unsurvivable cold with none of their clothing or supplies? Given that the incident occurred on the side of a snowy mountain, an easy explanation would be that the tent was hit by a sudden avalanche. However, recall that the first investigators on the scene, all of whom being experienced outdoorsmen and military servicemen possessing intimate familiarity with avalanches, did not see any evidence of a recent avalanche when they first came across the remains of the tent. The lack of evidence for a traditional avalanche has baffled investigators for decades—however, in 2020, a new scientific inquiry into the circumstances surrounding the incident may shed new light on this theory. Following a reopening of the case by Russian authorities in 2019, a team of scientists from ETH Zurich in Switzerland—scientists with specific expertise in the study of avalanches—came up with a new variation on the theory. While the conditions around the tent at the time of its discovery do make a *traditional* avalanche an unlikely possibility, the team was able to highlight how a very specific type of avalanche, known as a "slab avalanche," could have formed and rendered the damage to the tent as it was found.

A "slab" avalanche occurs when a thick layer of snow builds up over a relatively small area. As further layers of snowfall on top of it, the layer is compressed into a thick, heavy slab, while the foundation on which the slab rests becomes weaker and weaker under the accumulated weight. Eventually, the foundation gives way, and the now-heavy slab of compacted snow falls as one single block, often with a great deal of force capable of inflicting heavy damage to anything below it. Researchers working on the case compared the damage that could potentially be caused by a slab avalanche to that inflicted in a head-on car crash.

What's more, weather reports from the area around Dyatlov Pass at the night of the incident *do* show conditions in which slab avalanches would be most likely to occur. Heavy snow and high, gale-force winds could likely cause the accumulation and compacting of thick layers of snow across the mountain slope in the areas above the treeline. What's more, the tent itself may have played a role in any resulting slab avalanche. Dyatlov and company, being experienced hikers, would have likely pitched their tent within a thick layer of snow as an added layer of protection against the heavy winds blowing around the mountain. However, this move, while normally an important survival mechanism, may have proven fatal in this instance. Not knowing that such a thick and heavy layer of snow was rapidly building up just above them, the expedition team could have driven their tent stakes into the weaker layer of soft snow below the heavier upper-layer. This would have weakened the foundation of the snow slab even further and eventually caused the entire slab to collapse upon their tent with the force of a car crash.

This impact could have potentially inflicted many of the injuries later found on the bodies, including broken ribs and cracked skulls. Additionally, the sudden impact may have led the hikers to believe that they were being hit with a more traditional avalanche, one involving a much larger displacement of loose snow over a much larger area. Ironically, if a slab avalanche *was* the cause of the initial damage, the danger would actually have passed once it hit, as slab avalanches, though having the potential to inflict a great deal of damage upon a small area, do not threaten a larger area of a mountain the way that normal avalanches do. However, if the hikers did not know this, they would have likely assumed that their lives were in immediate danger inside the tent. This would explain why they needed to frantically cut their way out of the tent and why they fled so quickly to the tree line—where they would be safer from normal avalanche forces—without even taking the time to get dressed or gather their gear.

Upon reaching the tree line and taking shelter around the pine tree, it's likely (according to this theory) that the group immediately sought to build a fire. One member would have had to climb the tree to gather suitable branches and sticks, explaining the evidence of human activity on the tree itself. Of course, even if they had managed to construct a fire, the brutal cold of the Ural winter night would still have proven too much for them, especially in such limited clothing. Krivonischenko and Doroshenko, the first two bodies found near the tree, would have been the first to succumb to hypothermia. Though any account of the remaining hikers' motivation would be purely speculative, it's considered likely that the group eventually realized that they were *not* in immediate danger of being hit by an avalanche as they understood it. However, in the darkness of night without any clear light sources and with visibility deteriorating in the wind and snow, the remaining seven would likely have gotten lost trying to find their way back to the warmth of the tent. During their desperate search, Dyatlov, Slobodin, and Kolmogorova would have also succumbed to the cold, leaving their bodies scattered in the areas between the tree and the tent as they were found.

Unable to find the tent, the remaining four—Thibeaux-Brignolles, Dubinina, Kolevatov, and Zolotaryov—may have attempted to dig themselves a shelter in the snow, seeking out the thicker snow layers in the ravine where their bodies were eventually located. Here, the account becomes somewhat murkier, given the fact that many of the case's strangest details arose from the state in which their bodies were found. However, some have speculated that, given the fact that the ravine into which they were digging contained a stream that remained unfrozen in the wintertime, they may have accidentally dug underneath the snow layer into the stream itself. This may have caused their attempt at a snow shelter to collapse on top of them and bury them underneath more than a meter of snow, and potentially causing the numerous internal injuries found on their bodies. The missing eyes and tongues from their faces may have simply decomposed naturally or else been eaten by scavenging animals from the surrounding forest.

This account, plus or minus a few details, was officially accepted by the Russian authorities following their reopening of the case in 2019. A slightly alternate theory, one which has been somewhat absorbed into the main one, brings up the additional possibility of what is known as "katabatic winds." Katabatic winds are a type of powerful downdraft that brings a large quantity of dense, high-pressure air from a higher altitude to a lower altitude. These kinds of winds, most common among mountains, glaciers, and other types of elevated structures, can appear suddenly and produce immediate, hurricane-force winds on anything below them. Some scientists have speculated that a sudden katabatic wind descending rapidly from the mountain's summit could also explain the damage to the tent, as well as the group's sudden fleeing into the bitterly cold night. Katabatic winds could also produce a slab avalanche in the correct conditions, meaning that both explanations could, in fact, be true.

Of course, this account does *not* explain the elevated levels of radiation found on some of the bodies. Some later investigations have apparently found evidence that one or more of the expedition members had worked in a nuclear power plant just before embarking on the hike. However, even if this were the case, their radiation levels at the start of the expedition would have likely needed to be *much* higher than the normal contamination levels of most nuclear power plant employees, given the amount of time that had passed before the final four bodies were discovered, and given that they had spent more than two months lying within moving water (which would, according to experts, have likely washed away much of the radiation that was on the bodies initially). Plus, even with a slab avalanche, katabatic winds, and/or collapsing snow structure, many of the more severe injuries found on the bodies are still difficult to fully explain. Thus, though this "official" explanation was sufficient for Russian authorities, many around the world who have studied this case in depth remain unconvinced.

Therefore, we must now get into some of the more prevalent "alternate" theories of what happened in the Dyatlov Pass in February of 1959. Barring purely natural explanations, perhaps the most popular alternate theories involve covert activities and coverups by the Soviet military and/or KGB. The presence of radiation on some of the bodies has led some to the notion that the group had accidentally wandered into the site of a top-secret Soviet nuclear test. The shockwave of a nuclear explosion could have inflicted the kind of damage found on the tent and perhaps even convinced the experienced hikers that they were being hit with an avalanche or some other deadly force. This also would explain the radiation found on some of the bodies.

Of course, records recovered following the collapse of the Soviet Union show no evidence of any such test in that area of the Ural Mountains in 1959 or at any other time. Given that most of the Soviet Union's successful nuclear tests were eventually published in some form or another, it is unclear why such a test in the remote Ural wilderness would be covered up so thoroughly. Unless, of course, it was not merely a nuclear bomb but a *new* kind of experimental weapon that was being tested. Here, the theory falls into the realm of pure speculation, with some suggesting various types of experimental weapons technologies ranging from gamma-ray guns to sonic weapons and even weather-control machines. Of course, no evidence of any such tests has ever been uncovered, so if the Soviet Union *was* using the region around Kholat Syakhl for the testing of highly experimental weapons, they also did an excellent job of covering their tracks, at least so far.

When exploring the angle of potential KGB involvement, many amateur investigators have turned their attention to one particular member of the group. Semyon Zolotaryov had always stood out somewhat when browsing the complete manifest of expedition members. At age 38, Zolotaryov was much older than the other members of the group, all of whom were young university students in their early-20s. Despite intensive investigations in the years following the incident, the exact reason why Zolotaryov was included in the trip in the first place has never been made entirely clear. It seems as if he was added to the expedition at something of the last minute by the local sports committee. Accounts seem to suggest that he *may* have been originally scheduled to go on a different expedition sponsored by the committee but needed to pull out for unclear reasons and was subsequently placed with the Dyatlov group as a last-minute alternate.

However, attempts to get more information about Zolotaryov's past have turned up even more questions. A veteran of World War II, Zolotaryov appears to have gone off the grid somewhat for many of the 15 years between the end of the war and his death on the side of the mountain. With limited records of his life, many have speculated that he was, in fact, working with the KGB. Would this have some relation to the events of the night that he and the other eight hikers met their deaths? Perhaps, some have speculated, the area in which the hikers were planning to travel was, in fact, being used by the KGB or military for top-secret purposes, and Zolotaryov had been surreptitiously placed with them as a precautionary measure. If the group had indeed seen something that they were not meant to, the KGB could theoretically have "silenced" them to prevent these top-secret activities from getting out. But, if this were the case, why would Zolotaryov *also* be killed? Was he a loose end who needed to be sacrificed by his comrades for the greater good of the project's secrecy? Had he made some fatal mistake or error in judgment during the course of his covert activities that led to his untimely death?

Given that 1959 coincided with the height of Cold War tensions between the Soviet Union and the United States, some have also speculated that the *Americans* could be somehow involved in the tragedy. On the American side of things, contemporary records do show that '59 was around when the United States government was beginning to invest heavily in experimental weapons and reconnaissance technologies, which would eventually culminate in things like the now-famous U2 spy planes. Was this incident the result of a CIA or U.S. Army test of an experimental weapons system in the remote Soviet wilderness? As with the Soviet Union, no records have yet been uncovered from the CIA, U.S. military, or any other realm of the American government that would suggest such a thing. But, of course, much relating to American military and espionage activities during the Cold War remains highly classified, perhaps even more than is *unclassified*. Given this, some have even speculated that Zolotaryov, the odd-man out of the group, may have himself been a double-agent working for the CIA. If this is the case, his discovery by Soviet authorities may have led to his eventual death alongside the other eight members of the expedition. Of course, this theory would also raise far more questions than answers.

One other theory that was proposed early on in the initial investigation was that the group might have been attacked by the region's indigenous Mansi people. Undoubtedly, prejudices against such a remote and insular group played a major role in this. However, though this lead was pursued somewhat, investigators did not find any evidence of any kind of altercation or struggle between different people, and no incriminating evidence against any of the Mansi who lived nearby was ever found.

This leads us to the final and most outlandish class of theory on this case: that the "compelling natural force" that brought about the deaths of nine young hikers was, in fact, not of this "natural" world at all. Though one cannot say with certainty how quickly the UFO explanation took hold among some investigators following the incident itself, in subsequent years, the Dyatlov Pass deaths have come to be held up by ufologists and others as a potential example of a significant (and deadly) encounter between human beings and an alien race. These theories tend to be bolstered by unconfirmed reports of UFO sightings in that area of the Ural Mountains around the time of the incident itself. Additionally, the still-unexplained presence of radiation on some of the bodies may also be explained by an encounter with an extra-terrestrial craft.

    And this perhaps underscores the reason *why* this case still captivates so many minds more than half a century later. The incident was tragic enough—nine young and enthusiastic students and hikers were cut down by a mysterious calamity in the prime of their lives. The remote setting in the rugged and mysterious forests of the Ural Mountains adds even more strange gravitas to the situation. And then add in the bizarre and unsettling details—the severe injuries, the missing facial features, the radiation—and we have a case that continues to defy satisfactory explanation to this day. Although the case is "officially" settled, at least according to Russian authorities, this will not likely prevent speculation and conspiracy theories from growing and multiplying with each passing year. Ultimately, regardless of what facts are uncovered, what experiments are performed, or what experts are consulted, the ultimate, unchanging fact of the case may just be that the truth of what happened to those nine men and women on that cold night in February of 1959 may forever lie alongside them, yet another dead victim claimed by the snows and forests of Kholat Syakhl—the Dead Mountain.

Chapter 8
The Flannan Isles Lighthouse Disappearances

Scattered among the various corners of the Earth are a few wayward locations that, should the supernatural or otherworldly exist and commune with our space and time, would surely lay a strong claim to being one of its preeminent hideaways. Or, should the human mind bear the capacity to project secret nuances and pathologies unseen by our waking consciousness, would surely lay claim to being one of the deeper receptacles into which we may project our most feared and mythical archetypes. Among the locations that fit this description, few stand out quite so much as the strange, seemingly otherworldly islands that dot the cold North Atlantic off the western coast of Scotland. The product of primordial volcanic forces crudely crammed into the rest of the British Isles eons before human eyes had evolved to witness it, the islands surrounding Scotland appear to many observers to be the least "Earth-like" places to be nonetheless found on the Earth itself. Often barren of recognizable flora, save for the hardiest of grasses, moss, and shrubs, and defined by exotic geology carved by geothermal forces and the sea itself, Scotland's islands are, by the most conservative appraisals, striking enough to stupefy even the most rational and scientific minds.

Thus, wanderers should not be surprised that the few people who have lived and worked in these islands have in their collective consciousness generations-worth of stories of supernatural beings, fairies, and sprites, both playful and malevolent, conjured from water and the ground and the strange air itself. Unsurprisingly, few of the denizens of Scotland's outer coastline wish to stay too long on many of these islands or venture onto them after dark or during the cold and sunless depths of winter.

And cast off from these already cast off clusters of rock are the Flannan Isles. Lying along the western-most edge of the Outer Hebrides, the Flannan Isles, on a surface glance, may not seem particularly useful for much other than legend and landmarking. Indeed, this latter purpose led to the particular isle of Eilean Mòr being chosen as the location for a lighthouse towards the end of the 19th Century.

Knowing this, a visitor will probably find little shock to learn that one of the most mysterious and enduring mysteries from the history of the British Isles happened to occur here, among the barren rocks and stone, the frenzied sea mist, among the bleak midwinter cold and dark.

Completed in 1899, the Flannan Isles lighthouse on Eilean Mòr was likely already a strange and somewhat foreboding destination even when it was newly built. Perched atop one of Eilean Mòr's rocky hilltops, the lighthouse overlooks not only the sea but also a few mysterious and ancient stone ruins, the remnants of early Christian chapels dedicated to the eponymous St Flannan over a millennium ago.

And, of course, it would only take a little over a year following its completion for it to see the haunting mystery that has since made it one of the most infamous lighthouses in the world.

Operating under the authority of Scotland's Northern Lighthouse Board, the Flannan Isles lighthouse was meant to be manned by a three-person team throughout its first few years of operation. This team would normally be composed of a senior keeper and two junior keepers, each of whom would (in theory) follow specified safety protocols in the event of an emergency or security incident. In the year 1900, the first full year of the lighthouse's operation, the crew manifest had been designed to allow for a rotating team of keepers, with each man in the crew working six-week stints on the island and then taking two weeks off while his place would be taken by another crew member rotated in.

In December of 1900, the three-man team working on Eilean Mòr was 43-year-old senior keeper James Ducat, as well as the two assistant keepers, 28-year-old Thomas Marshall and 40-year-old Donald MacArthur.

One potential cause for concern on the remote island—which would, later on, bear significant consequences for the subsequent mystery that was to unfold—was the lack of reliable communication between the lighthouse and the mainland. In 1900, radio—then still an infant technology—had not yet made its way to the network of lighthouses along the Scottish coast, and the rough maritime terrain of the Outer Hebrides made it virtually impossible to set up reliable telegraph lines. Thus, should the lighthouse keepers on Eilean Mòr need to communicate an emergency or concern to their superiors, their only means of doing so was via visual signals. Specifically, a gamekeeper stationed on a nearby island was paid a fairly meager sum of £8 per year to keep watch towards the lighthouse for any signal of distress or other communication from the keepers stationed there. In practice, the keepers were instructed to employ their flag, or a large ball hung from the lighthouse top, in order to get the game keeper's attention. The gamekeeper, in turn, was meant to relay this to the Northern Lighthouse Board authorities, who would then dispatch assistance to the island.

Due to this dearth in communication, we who are investigating this case today have little to no direct information regarding not only the events that would subsequently occur but also the day-to-day activities, thoughts, and mood of the three men tasked with spending that bleak December out on a forlorn rock in the North Sea. What limited insights contemporary investigators have come from the sparse and somewhat cryptic journal logs kept by the keepers over the course of the first few weeks of December. Ostensibly, this log was intended merely to keep track of lighthouse activity, weather, tasks assigned to each individual keeper, and other mundane bits and pieces of information that would need to be catalogued for posterity's sake. But, in some cases, the inner mood of the men working on the lighthouse seemed to come out in subtle ways, even as they described some of the more boring aspects of their day-to-day job.

Undoubtedly the combination of climate, location, and time of year was wearing down the spirits of Ducat, Marshall, and MacArthur. With a shift that was scheduled to see them through the entire month of December, all three men were looking at spending Christmas away from their families, with only the company of two other burly men and the cold December elements. Indeed, various journal logs suggest as much, with Ducat describing a somber mood that had descended upon the team.

Nothing was *obviously* amiss on Eilean Mòr until the evening of December 15. On that day, the *SS Archtor*, an American ship sailing from Philadelphia to the Port of Leith, passed by the Flannan Isles at some point after sundown. The captain of the vessel made a note that the lighthouse on Eilean Mòr was strangely out, a notable occurrence among the normally reliable lighthouses that dotted the coasts of Scotland and the Northern U.K. This was particularly ominous as the ship had logged some rough weather in the area the past few days, and the crew of the *Archtor* worried that a lack of clear light on the Flannans may lead to future catastrophes at sea. Upon reaching their destination at Leith, the captain of the *Archtor* reported the absence of light on Eilean Mòr to the Northern Lighthouse Board. However, as no remote communication yet existed between the island and the mainland, the Lighthouse Board Authorities had no immediate means to get in touch with the three men who were supposed to be stationed there.

Even worse, the inclement weather proved a significant impediment to getting relief vessels to the island in person. This was particularly unfortunate a few days later. Initially, the fourth keeper—Joseph Moore—was meant to sail to Eilean Mòr on December 20, a mere five days after the *Archtor* noted the absence of light on the island. As per the schedule in place, Moore was set to rotate into his next shift on the 20th, relieving the occasional keeper MacArthur, who himself was already working a longer than normal shift as a replacement for another keeper on extended sick leave. However, rough weather and rougher seas forced Moore and the Northern Lighthouse Board authorities to postpone their journey to the island by several days. Thus, it was not until December 26, Boxing Day, that Moore and several seamen were able to depart from the mainland, onboard a ship called the *Hesperus*, to try and make contact with the three men on Eilean Mòr and determine what, if anything, had occurred.

One might stop and imagine the slow burn of dread that built in the minds of the men on board that ship, especially Joseph Moore himself. Moore was, after all, not only a co-worker but a friend and colleague of the three men whom he was meant to relieve on that desolate island. Knowing their experience and professionalism in the roles as lighthouse keepers, Moore would also have difficulty conceiving that the highly-experienced James Ducat and the adept MacArthur and Marshall would simply be so careless as to let the crucial light go out in a dark December evening, especially when the elements had turned as foul as they were the night that the *Archtor* passed by. Moore, however, may have nonetheless sought to try and convince himself of that prospect during the entire voyage to the island, no matter how little it squared with his understanding of three men. The alternatives, of course, were much worse.

Although the weather had settled enough to allow the *Hesperus* to set sail, the sea, and sky no doubt continued to bear the bleak and ominous darkness of December in the North Atlantic, elements that surely must have flamed the growing dread that Moore and the others felt. According to some reports from the ship's crew, Moore himself refrained from eating during the entire voyage to the island, preferring to only drink coffee to keep himself awake and rarely speaking with anyone else.

As the *Hesperus* approached the island, the crew immediately saw unavoidable signs that something was indeed wrong at the lighthouse. The captain of the *Hesperus*, Jim Harvie, noted that the lighthouse's flag pool had no flag affixed to its mast, contrary to general protocols. What's more, a pile of provision boxes had been left on the island's landing rather than being restocked. But, most ominously, none of the three keepers were waiting at the landing to greet the ship. In an attempt at communication, Captain Harvie blew the ship's horn to try and get the attention of whoever may be inside the lighthouse. When that failed to produce any response, the ship's crew fired a flare over the building, as if the problem was merely visual. Once again, the island responded with no sign of human life, only the cold howling of the wind and the ever-present sound of waves crashing against the jagged rocks along the shore.

Moore, being the relief keeper most acquainted with the island and the three men stationed there, was sent ashore on a smaller boat, docking at the island's east landing and making his way towards the lighthouse. There, he made a strange discovery. Not only was the front gate of the property still closed, but the front door and vestibule door of the lighthouse building itself was also properly closed. Entering the building, Moore began searching through the various rooms for any sign of things amiss. Initially, his search did not produce much out of the ordinary. Most of the furniture and stored items were in their proper place. The fireplace was cold, signifying that it had not been lit in several days. The beds in the sleeping quarters were unmade as if their respective bodies were planning on returning soon enough. Throughout the lighthouse, Moore did not find any obvious sign of anything particularly strange or foreboding.

That is, except for the small matter that the three keepers were nowhere to be found.

Following his initial search, Moore returned to the *Hesperus* to report his findings, soon after returning with two other able-bodied seamen to go about both a more thorough search and the still-crucial task of getting the light back into working order. With Moore and the volunteers going back to the island, Captain Davie sent a telegram to the Northern Lighthouse Board, which stated:

> A dreadful accident has happened at the Flannans. The three keepers, Ducat, Marshall and the Occasional have disappeared from the Island... The clocks were stopped and other signs indicated that the accident must have happened about a week ago. Poor fellows, they must have been blown over the cliffs or drowned trying to secure a crane.

Meanwhile, Moore and the volunteers were able to get the main light up and running without much difficulty. With that matter resolved, they were then able to go about a more thorough search of the lighthouse and surrounding island. During this more extensive search, a few small but ominous details did turn up. Though no sign of any of the three men were anywhere to be found, nor did the lighthouse's interior show any clear signs of a violent struggle, a few things *were* out of place here and there. For one, Moore noticed that a chair in the dining area had been overturned. Even more strangely, two of the three oilskin coats kept in the lighthouse were missing, but a third remained hanging where it would have been left. Moore identified this oilskin as belonging to Donald MacArthur, meaning that, if MacArthur was still alive somewhere, he would be braving the cold elements of a North Atlantic December without adequate clothing.

What's more, as the captain's telegram had suggested, all of the clocks inside the lighthouse were found to have stopped. These being more antiquated mechanical clocks, the fact that they were stopped is not *so* unusual, save for the fact that it indicated a somewhat prolonged absence of any person around to tend to them.

With the lighthouse up and running, Moore and the other volunteer keepers then had the unenviable task of remaining on the island by themselves, waiting several days in isolation for the *Hesperus* and other ships to return with more supplies and a better equipped investigative body from the Northern Lighthouse Board. Here, imagination can suffice for how unsettling the scenario must have been. While Moore and his team of volunteer keepers must have known the importance of going about their duties, keeping the light illuminated, and maintaining the facility in working order, the dark elements of the situation must have impressed upon them. As anyone tasked with tending that particular lighthouse would already know, the simple fact of the climate, the cold, overcast skies, the limited sunlight and extended darkness of December, and the perpetual hypnotic effects of the sea were, in and of themselves, often enough to produce an unsettling effect on the minds of even the most seasoned seamen. But add in the *disappearance* and the strange, nearly incomprehensible nature of three capable men seemingly vanishing without a trace, the scene unfolded before Moore, and the others would have inspired far darker and more foreboding feelings. Perhaps, as they went about their tasks, their minds began returning to those old myths and legends that had long surrounded the islands. The folklore whispered by the inhabitants of the isolated Hebrides islands, speaking of strange, supernatural beings, water sprites and fairies, ghosts and demonic entities that rose from the sea or rode invisibly upon the air, and who regarded the race of men with a mischievous malevolence, or, worse, an outright hostility. Did Moore and the others, stranded by themselves upon the island, find themselves turning with more alarm at every sound that echoed around them? Every crash of wave against a rock, every sudden shriek of the wind, every shudder of the lighthouse's foundations?

With the lighthouse up and running once again, Moore had time to engage in a more thorough search of the island as he waited for reinforcements to arrive. While his initial search of the lighthouse itself had not turned up much save for a few out-of-place items of clothing and an overturned chair, a more extended exploration of the grounds did turn up more intriguing and ominous findings. Moore had docked on the island at its east landing, where everything was more or less as it should have been. However, as he ventured out to the western landing on the opposite side of the island, he found a different story. The western landing *did* show signs of having suffered significant damage from an unknown cause. The iron railings leading down the path to the dock had been bent, and in a few places, dislodged entirely from the ground. What's more, a tackle box suspended about 33 meters, or 108 feet, over the cliffside was knocked over, and its contents were strewn across the path. Moore, an experienced keeper, well acquainted with the elements in the Outer Hebrides, likely found pause in considering this damage. The weather had indeed been rough in the weeks leading up to his arrival on the island, so much so that his journey had been postponed several days to wait for the seas to calm. But even so, for winds or waves to inflict *that* kind of damage on supposedly firm iron and concrete fixtures would suggest severe weather of a kind that was beyond even the storms of the past few weeks. Or, at least, the storms that Moore and the others had experienced back on the Scottish mainland. Had Eilean Mòr somehow experienced a freak weather phenomenon localized to the island itself but not extending far beyond the Flannans? Standing at that western landing, Moore would have most likely heard only the wind and the waves providing an answer.

A few days later, on December 29 (and, one imagines, much to the relief of Moore and the volunteer crew), assistance finally arrived in the form of Northern Lighthouse Board superintendent Robert Muirhead, who arrived with additional personnel to conduct an official inquiry into the disappearance. Like Joseph Moore, Muirhead had a personal as well as an official motivation for his presence in the inquiry. As superintendent, Muirhead had personally hired all three missing men and knew them well. Not only that, but Muirhead is believed to have been the last person to see all three men alive, having gone to the island himself on official business a few weeks before their disappearance.

After searching over the entire island as thoroughly as possible—and still finding no sign of any of the three keepers or any other potential clues as to what could have happened to them—Muirhead and the Northern Lighthouse Board investigators turned to their only other potential source of information. Recall that, since Eilean Mòr was cut off from telegraph and radio communication to the mainland due to its remote location, the only means that the men stationed there had of communicating any potential distress to the outside world was through visual signals to the nearest inhabited island. The closest person who would have had constant visual contact with the light itself and who could have seen any distress signal from the island was the gamekeeper on Gallan Head, a promontory on the nearby Isle of Lewis, about 18 miles southeast of Eilean Mòr. Here, gamekeeper Roderick Mackenzie had received a small salary of about £8 per year from the Lighthouse Board to keep watch for any sign of distress or to report if the light had gone out for an extended period of time. Thus, Mackenzie was one of the first people to be contacted by the Board's investigation following the discovery of the men's disappearance.

Mackenzie, however, proved to be less than helpful. According to his account, he had not seen any specific distress signal from the island that may have signified that the three keepers were in any kind of danger. However, he *did* report that, from his vantage point, the light from the lighthouse had been out for around two weeks prior to Moore and company relighting it. Mackenzie estimated that he had last seen the light around December 12, around three days before the *Archtor* passed by the darkened light on the 15th. However, despite receiving a salary from the Board for exactly this purpose, Mackenzie had *not* reported this to anyone.

Mackenzie's failure here bears something of a tragic irony to the case. Some reports have indicated that Ducat, as the lighthouse's principal keeper, had, in fact, earlier requested that the Lighthouse Board conduct an experiment, whereby the men stationed on the island would send out a visual distress signal of some sort, and then see how long it would take for someone to notice and report it to the proper board authorities. This particular experiment was never actually authorized, so it never ended up being performed. However, given Mackenzie's dereliction of his duty and failure to immediately telegraph the absence of the light until it was well too late, some may say that Ducat was ultimately shown to be correct in his concern.

Muirhead's eventual conclusion following his more detailed investigation became the "official" conclusion on the matter taken by the Northern Lighthouse Board, which it still holds to this day. One of the core questions pertaining to the disappearance of all *three* men was why the lighthouse itself was left unattended. Lighthouse protocols set by the Northern Lighthouse Board strictly reinforced the requirement that at no time should a lighthouse be left unattended. Thus, if two of the keepers needed to venture out onto the island for any reason, protocol would necessitate that one be left behind to man the lighthouse. Muirhead also noted that James Ducat, the head keeper, had more than twenty years of experience and was well familiar with the rules governing lighthouse maintenance.

Ultimately, Muirhead's conclusion was derived from two main pieces of evidence: the damage to the western landing and the oilskin coat left inside the lighthouse. As the coat that had been left behind was determined to have belonged to Donald MacArthur, Muirhead arrived at the following scenario as being most likely. Rough weather, probably taking the form of heavy winds and larger than normal waves, had caused damage to the western landing, upending the railing and scattering supplies from the tackle box along the path. Noticing the damage, Ducat and Marshall had likely ventured out to gather whatever supplies they could and try to fix the damage, taking their oilskin coats and other relevant items of protective clothing with them as they braved the elements. MacArthur, as per protocol, remained inside to man the light itself.

However, as they worked precariously close to the cliffside overlooking the island's western coastline, some sort of natural force—either a large, rogue wave, a sudden gale force wind or some combination of the two—struck Ducat and Marshall and swept them off the cliffside into the tempestuous ocean below. MacArthur, either seeing this himself from inside the lighthouse or being alerted by their cries for help, abandoned his post and ran outside to try and rescue them. Though MacArthur *did* have several years of experience working lighthouses and was familiar with the rules prohibiting such abandonment, the official report did note that MacArthur was, in fact, an *occasional* keeper, who was then filling in for another crew member on sick leave. The fact that MacArthur had less full-time experience as a lighthouse keeper, combined with some second-hand reports of his surlier and more troublesome personality, possibly made it more likely that *he* would be the one to disregard an important protocol like that in the event of an emergency. Thus, according to this theory, MacArthur rushed outside to the aid of his fellow keepers in such a hurry that he knocked over the overturned chair in the dining area and did not even have time or thought to put his oilskin on. Once at the western landing, however, MacArthur befell the same fate as Ducat and Marshall, either being swept into the sea by another rogue wave, being pulled in by a rope he had thrown to them, or falling in as he tried to navigate the steep and slippery rocks of the cliffside.

Thus, in his official report on the incident, Muirhead wrote:

> From evidence which I was able to procure I was satisfied that the men had been on duty up till dinner time on Saturday the 15th of December, that they had gone down to secure a

box in which the mooring ropes, landing ropes etc. were kept, and which was secured in a crevice in the rock about 110 feet above sea level, and that an extra-large sea had rushed up the face of the rock, had gone above them, and coming down with immense force, had swept them completely away.

This report was accepted by the Northern Lighthouse Board, and to this day, remains the "official" explanation for the disappearance of the three men. However, this account is *not* without issues. One of the details that lingers the most in the face of explanation was the state of the lighthouse gate and door. Recall that when Joseph Moore finally returned to Eilean Mòr on December 26—apparently the first person to do so following the disappearance—he found the outer gate of the facility, the lighthouse's front door, *and* the inner vestibule door all to be securely closed. This detail does not correspond to a scenario in which the last person to leave the lighthouse was doing so in a panicked rush in the face of an emergency situation. After all, if MacArthur was in such a rush to rescue his two fallen comrades that he did not even think to put on his coat as he ventured out into the cold and windy December evening, *why* then would he take the time to close all three doors behind him?

Another issue stems from the *timing* of the supposed incident that swept all three men out to sea. Based upon the state of things inside the lighthouse at the time of the disappearance, the weather reports, and the last logs in the keeper's records, Muirhead estimated that the damage to the western landing and attempt at a repair by Ducat and Marshall had likely occurred during the evening. This, however, did not correspond to what would likely have been the standard procedure and basic common sense for experienced lighthouse keepers. Ducat, with more than twenty years of experience working both the Eilean Mòr lighthouse and other lighthouses in similar terrain, would be well aware of the dangers of working so close to the cliffside, especially during inclement weather, and especially near or after dark. Though the damage to the western landing would have needed to be dealt with eventually, there was no reason why Ducat would have felt the need to do so exactly then. Many other lighthouse keepers came to the same conclusion: an experienced keeper like Ducat would have likely determined it to be too dangerous to attempt to deal with the damage to the western landing in dark and stormy conditions like that and would instead have made the call to hold off any repairs until morning, under much calmer weather conditions. To make such a reckless, and frankly stupid, call as that was, by all accounts, quite out of character for the professional and experienced Ducat.

But another even more problematic detail was found in the official logs kept by the keepers before their disappearance. In one of his official reports several days before the incident, Ducat specifically noted the damage to the western landing as having already occurred. Thus, while it appears likely that this damage *was* done by inclement weather or rough seas, it seems to have happened at least *several days* before the three keepers went missing. If this were the case, Ducat's apparent decision to attempt repairs in the stormy evening of the 15th makes even *less* sense, as the crew had several prior days of better light and better conditions to make the necessary repairs.

Another potential issue was the fact that no trace of any of the three bodies was ever found. Of course, the ocean is vast, and if all three men were, in fact, swept out to sea, it's entirely possible that they were simply lost in the massive expanse of the water. However, many people familiar with the Flannan Isles and the Outer Hebrides have noted that the specific currents and tides that surround the islands make it more likely that objects that fall in the water around the islands will tend to wash upon them eventually. Thus, if Ducat, Marshall, and MacArthur had, in fact, fallen to their deaths from Eilean Mòr's western cliffside, the tide *should* still have produced their bodies back onto the island's shoreline to be eventually found during the subsequent investigation.

Finally, there remains the issue of what kind of wave could have potentially washed the three men off the safety of the island and into the unforgiving ocean. Keep in mind, the cliff overlooking the western landing was around 33 meters—or 110 feet—high. Thus, any wave that could have swept the men away would have needed to be *at least* that high (and likely even higher in order to generate enough force at the top of the cliff to wash the men off their feet). While the seas surrounding the island can, in fact, get quite rough, a 33-meter wave is more or less unheard of around the Hebrides. Even in the worst storms, no lighthouse keeper or sailor had ever recorded anywhere near a 33-meter wave in the vicinity of the island.

Thus, while Muirhead's explanation of a tragic accident due to bad conditions and bad decisions was sufficient for the "official" report of the Northern Lighthouse Board, enough strange and unexplained details linger on to keep questions and dissatisfaction burning in the minds of many of the three men's colleagues, as well as many of those who live and work in and around the mysterious and isolated islands of the Outer Hebrides.

Another theory that has been proposed posits more personal causes of the tragedy. After all, if one is inclined to disregard nature as the cause of the men's disappearances, the only other "rational" option would be the men themselves. Given the extreme isolation of the environment, where the men were deprived of even communication by telegram for weeks at a time, some have speculated that one or more of the three keepers may have suffered from some kind of mental breakdown. If this were the case, it is possible that this man may have murdered his two fellow keepers in a fit of isolation-induced madness, disposing of their bodies by throwing them into the sea. Then, still in the grips of madness, or else realizing what he had done and unable to live with himself, he took his own life by jumping from the cliff and joining his two comrades in the cold and unsettled sea.

Proponents of this theory most often point to Donald MacArthur as the most likely culprit. MacArthur, after all, was only the occasional keeper, who had been forced to remain on the island for a much longer period than his shifts would normally require due to another assistant keeper being informed on an extended sick leave. Some reports have painted a psychological profile of MacArthur in which he bore a somewhat violent temper and generally, surely, gruff attitude. This theory is also potentially bolstered by the fact that Robert Muirhead, the Northern Lighthouse Board superintendent, had made a personal visit to Eilean Mòr several weeks before the disappearance of the three men. While Muirhead only noted this fact to draw attention to the melancholy conclusion that he was the last person to see the three men alive, later commentators have pointed out that it is somewhat odd for a man with such as high position in the Board to be making personal calls to remote lighthouses of this nature. While Muirhead was, in fact, well-acquainted with all three men, perhaps even considering them "friends," the fact remains that the official duties of the Northern Lighthouse Board superintendent do *not* usually include taking the long journey from the Board's central offices in Edinburgh to the highly remote and isolated Flannan Islands, *unless* something was significantly amiss.

Some have speculated that the purpose of this visit was, in actuality, to deal with a personal issue that may have arisen among the three keepers. Specifically, some have speculated that the surly and ill-tempered MacArthur may have become gravely upset that his shift on the island had been extended so dramatically from what he had initially signed up to work. This speculation further extends to the theory that Ducat and Marshall may have grown so concerned with MacArthur's increasingly aggressive or unsettling behaviour that they themselves requested that Muirhead come to the island personally to try and reassure MacArthur that his shift on the island would not be significantly extended beyond December of 1900. Of course, Muirhead himself makes no mention of this anywhere in his official account, and while specific reports on MacArthur's character may vary in accuracy, everything else is purely speculative, with little to no concrete evidence to support it.

The other flaw with this theory is, of course, the lack of any clear indication of a violent struggle. Aside from the single overturned chair, nothing within the lighthouse was noticeably amiss during the initial investigation. Given that all three men were strong enough to meet the physical demands of the job, a violent struggle between them would likely have produced much greater damage and havoc within the house.

So, with both "natural" explanations having some degree of problems, we must therefore now turn to the "supernatural" explanations that have since been put forth for the strange disappearance of three grown men. Unsurprisingly, given the location itself, the most popular of these "alternative" explanations centers around the dark and macabre mythology associated with the islands themselves. As previously stated, the residents of the Hebrides have, for millennia, told tales of strange, supernatural entities that supposedly haunt these islands and the sea surrounding them. Traditional Scottish folklore has for ages told tales of mischievous, and in some cases malevolent, fairy entities that can sometimes take a malign interest in the affairs of humankind. Going back to the earliest records from the various peoples inhabiting Scotland, investigators can find numerous cases of missing persons that were explained by means of a malign encounter with one of these beings, who can (supposedly) use their magical power to lure men to their deaths, or into perpetual imprisonment within the fairy's hidden land.

Around the isles of the Hebrides, this kind of traditional folklore unsurprisingly took a specifically nautical turn. One of the more prominent tales told by the inhabitants of the Hebrides is that of the so-called "Blue Men of the Minch." These beings, who are also sometimes referred to as "Storm Kelpies," are often described as a kind of "water sprite," or essentially a "mer-person," resembling humans in some regard, but also being distinguished by blue skin, some fish-like features, and, of course, the fact that they live under the straits separating the Hebrides from mainland Scotland. Though tales regarding these beings tend to vary somewhat in details, common themes include their supposed ability to create storms and their penchant for attempting to sink passing ships.

Within the context of this broader mythology, the Flannan Isles themselves possessed a particular reputation among the locals even before the disappearance of the three keepers. For years, shepherds on the nearby islands would bring sheep to graze on the islands during the day, drawn by legends that the grass and elements of the islands possessed some kind of magical property that would heal sick or injured sheep who grazed there, or induce ewes to give birth to twins during future mating seasons. Of course, these voyages during the island *only* took place under the daylight. The shepherds who brought their sheep to graze on the islands always made sure to keep a steady watch on the location of the sun in the western sky, taking care to set off the islands while there was still daylight, and never to get caught there after dark. Perhaps these long-time residents of the Hebrides knew of the potential for supernatural threats without the protection of the sunlight, and maybe had even heard whispers that the very same "blue men" who resided under the waves of the Minch may be bold enough to venture onto land in these isolated islands. Here, they would, in turn, be unlikely to take kindly to any human souls who dared venture onto *their* land after dark.

Given how far these stories stretched back into the centuries, it should come as no surprise that muted whispers began to arise among the native Hebrideans about what *really* happened to James Ducat, Donald MacArthur, and Thomas Marshall. Had they, in fact, fallen victim to a race of supernatural, elemental beings that resided under the waves surrounding Eilean Mòr?

Strangely, one of the consistent themes surrounding the various legends of the "blue men" is that, should one find oneself under attack from them, the only true defence is to defeat them in a so-called "rhyming duel." This, of course, plays in with broader Scottish tradition. Going back to the Middle Ages, and perhaps even earlier, residents of the Scottish Highlands and Islands were known to engage in a practice commonly known as "flyting," in which two or more aggrieved parties would take turns trading insults by means of off-the-cuff rhymes. Though this tradition died out among Scotland's human population some time ago, the practice supposedly remains an effective defence against a blue man attack. One particular tale, well-known to residents of the Hebrides, details the captain of a ship who, when facing an attack by a hostile group of blue men who sought to capsize his ship and drag him and his crew down to the ocean depths, was able to mount a successful defence by exchanging rhymed insults with the blue man king. The king, unable to respond to the quick-witted captain's taunts, became unable to conjure his sea magic against the ship and was forced to call a humiliating retreat back into the waves.

Of course, neither Ducat, Marshall, nor MacArthur was particularly known for their quick wits or verbal skills. Thus, if their lighthouse did indeed fall prey to an attack of malevolent blue men who rose from the ocean depths, they would have been unlikely to follow in that captain's footsteps and mount a successful rhyming defence of their island. Their disappearance, then, would have been the consequence of having to share their work and living quarters with such powerful supernatural beings, who were perhaps aggrieved that the islands which they had previously had all to themselves were now so rudely inhabited by man and his strange illuminated building.

One of the difficulties in developing sound theories as to the fate of the missing men is a notable lack of clarity on the veracity of certain pieces of information that tend to pop up during discussions of the case. Some supposed "facts" that often get mentioned may not have much evidence supporting them or, in some cases, may have been proven entirely fraudulent. Arguably the most troublesome of these factoids is the contents of the keeper's log that was found in the lighthouse following the men's disappearance. As per the official duties of the keepers, the men (most likely Ducat, the principal keeper who would have been tasked with such things) were to keep records of the schedule of the light's illumination, possible damages that would need to be repaired, barometric and meteorological readings, and other blander pieces of data that would be relevant to the maintenance of a lighthouse in general. However, in the decades following the disappearance, as the case grew in popularity as an "unsolved mystery," more and more accounts began to reference additional information found in these logs. According to these accounts, the last few entries left by the missing men began to include information beyond the basics of their jobs, referencing personal feelings of isolation, foreboding of the weather and the condition of the sea, and even the psychological state of the men themselves. Later accounts have referenced logs that mentioned frightful storms that hit the island in the days leading up to December 15, storms that, if these accounts are to be believed, instilled tremendous fear in all three keepers.

Most of these accounts assert that the logs in question were written not by Principal Keeper Ducat but rather by Second Assistant Keeper Thomas Marshall. Allegedly, Marshall himself wrote that the island encountered storms so bad that they "caused the men to pray." Marshall also began to note ominous changes in the mood of his co-workers, detailing a darker psychological state that seemed to have descended upon the island in the first few weeks of December. In these accounts, Marshall wrote that Principal Keeper Ducat had become "very quiet in recent days." Other accounts have Marshall writing that MacArthur, normally known for being gruff and surely, had "been seen crying," possibly out of distress from the barrage of storms, or possibly for some other reason. Finally, the last supposed Marshall entry in these logs, allegedly left a day or so before the men's disappearance, read: "Storm ended. Sea Calm. God is overall."

The description of violent storms and a deteriorating mental state among the lighthouse staff has served as evidence for both the official account of the disappearance (that the men were swept off the island in a rogue wave conjured by stormy seas) and the theory that one or more of the keepers suffered a mental breakdown, murdered his companions, and then killed himself. However, a more diligent inspection of these claims finds several holes in the "Marshall log" account. For one, no evidence of these additional logs can be found in any of the initial reports of the case. In fact, they do not appear until several decades later, being included in a sensationalized account of the disappearance found in an American tabloid in the 1930s. Given that this is not the most reputable source for such information, most serious investigators have dismissed these accounts as fake. Besides, the information contained in these accounts does not make much sense in the context of Marshall's position at the lighthouse or the purpose of the logs themselves. Bear in mind, Marshall was the *junior-most* member of the staff, and Ducat and MacArthur were his direct superiors. Even if he had noticed a darker change in mood among his co-workers, it would have been far out of line for him to use the official logs to record such personal and irrelevant information about his supervisors. Thus, though it may be tantalizing to turn to these supposed Marshall logs as an intriguing bit of evidence, a serious assessment of this case must ultimately dismiss them as a likely hoax.

Among all of the various accounts and retellings of the case, two other details are sometimes added to the story that we have reason to cast doubt upon. In one account, Moore and the other volunteers who first searched the lighthouse after the disappearance found the men's dinner still sitting on the kitchen table, half-eaten as if something had interrupted them in the middle of their evening meal. This detail has been used to try and support a few different theories, ranging from a sudden catastrophic wave big enough to reach the relative safety of the lighthouse's kitchen to a more macabre supernatural occurrence that caused the men to suddenly flee in terror. However, as with the Marshall logs, no contemporary evidence from the initial reports has ever been found indicating that half-eaten meals were found anywhere in the lighthouse.

Another story, one that is often used to try and support more supernatural explanations, involves Moore noticing three blackbirds flying from the top of the lighthouse when he first approached the building on December 26. Blackbirds of this kind are not native to or often seen on the Flannan Isles, so Moore's sighting of them would have proven a somewhat strange occurrence. Here, folklore and myth take hold somewhat, as more credulous interpreters of the case assert that these three blackbirds were, in fact, the three lighthouse keepers themselves. In this account, an enchantment of some kind—performed by water sprites, fairies, witches, or some other supernatural power associated with the island—cursed the men to be transformed into blackbirds, seeing their friend come to relieve them but unable to communicate in any meaningful way outside of incoherent squawks and caws. Of course, in addition to the numerous issues with this story in and of itself, the account of Moore seeing the three blackbirds has never been substantiated in any way, shape, or form, so contemporary investigators into this case have *at least* one reason to dismiss it.

In recent years, following the advent of the modern-day interest in UFOs and alien encounters, many people newly familiar with the case have theorized that alien abduction could be the cause of the disappearance. Little to no evidence exists for this hypothesis, however, save for a few minor details, such as the fact that all of the clocks in the lighthouse were stopped, a phenomenon sometimes reported with cases of supposed alien encounters (though, recall that these clocks were more antiquated wind-up clocks, which needed to be wound on occasion to remain functional. The absence of any keepers to do so would have resulted in all of them stopping on their own after a few days). A few later accounts of the disappearance have cited reports of strange lights in the sky over the Flannan Isles from residents of the nearby inhabited island. However, even less evidence exists to verify these accounts than the log entries supposedly left by Marshall, the half-eaten meals, or the sighting of three blackbirds, so they can perhaps reasonably be dismissed as fictitious.

Chapter 9
The Bridge at Overtoun That Calls Dogs to Their Maker

Staying in Scotland, we now move to a mystery that's a bit more contemporary but no less mysterious or ominous (at least if you're a dog-lover).

The Scottish town of Dumbarton, on the surface, does not appear to hold too many dark secrets. Located in West Dunbartonshire, about 21 kilometres southeast of Glasgow, Dumbarton looks like a fairly nondescript Scottish town lying between the River Clyde and the River Leven. And the source of the mystery that has made this town infamous in some circles is even less ostentatious on the surface level. The Overtoun Bridge certainly *looks* nice enough. Spanning the Overtoun Burn, the bridge leads to the eponymous Overtoun House, a picturesque 19th Century estate overlooking the banks of the River Clyde.

But, in keeping with its antiquated stone masonry and ominous, almost Gothic-like aesthetic, the Overtoun Bridge has over the past several decades developed a much darker reputation. But while readers may be unsurprised to read that the bridge has become an epicentre for a string of bizarre suicides and suicide attempts, the twist is that the victims of this bridge are not human at all.

Rather, Overtoun Bridge has achieved infamy around the world as the so-called "dog suicide bridge." As this title suggests, the bridge has become notable for the bizarre number of recorded instances in which dogs, seemingly drawn by some kind of force or impulse imperceptible to their human handlers, are compelled to suddenly bolt from the walkway and jump headfirst over the side of the bridge, into the waters of the Overtoun Burn below. Given the idyllic nature of the scenery, it should come as no surprise that many of the dog-owning residents of Dumbarton would choose the Overtoun House and surrounding grounds as a nice place to take their canine companions for a nice, relaxing walk. Of course, for many of those residents who were not acquainted with the bridge's sinister reputation, they may be likely to get a nasty surprise when they take their dog across the bridge.

The exact number of incidents in which dogs jumped from the bridge is difficult to determine. Investigators do believe that reports of dog "suicides" from the bridge go back to at least the 1950s and possibly earlier. As these cases grew more well-known around the world in the 2000s, official records began to tabulate around 50 dogs that jumped to their deaths from the bridge, and as many as 600 more that jumped but (thankfully) survived. Though most accounts of dog jumps are anecdotal, they do tend to follow the same pattern. A dog, normally one considered well-behaved or well-trained, will be walking quite constantly and obediently at the side of its own as the pair nears the Overtoun Bridge. Then, as they step onto the bridge, the dog will suddenly turn and run to the side of the bridge and jump off without any apparent hesitation, usually ignoring any calls or commands given by its startled owner.

Most of the specific cases that we know of coming from the mid-to-late-2000s when journalists and animal welfare organizations such as the Scottish Society for the Prevention of Cruelty to Animals began to investigate these cases more seriously. For example, most reports suggest that as many as five different dogs had jumped over the bridge in one six-month period in 2005. In one notable case from 2004, a local man named Kenneth Meikle was walking his beloved golden retriever over the bridge when the dog, apparently compelled by force beyond Meikle's comprehensive, suddenly and without warning bolted for the sidewalls of the bridge, jumping over them and into the waters below without any apparent fear or hesitation.

Fortunately, Meikle's dog survived the fall, though Meikle noted that it experienced what appeared to be a degree of "shock" and "trauma" at the experience. In another documented case from 2014, a local woman named Alice Trevorrow was walking her dog, a pet springer spaniel named Cassie, over the bridge when the dog began to act strangely. Although she was able to prevent Cassie from jumping, she did notice that the dog appeared to suddenly become agitated and fixated on something, behaviour that was apparently out of character for the normally well-behaved dog. When interviewed about the incident later, Trevorrow was quoted as saying: "Me and my son walked toward Cassie, who was staring at something above the bridge… she definitely saw something that made her jump. There is something sinister going on. It was so out of character for her."

The fact that this one single bridge has such a noticeable and disturbing effect on dogs—an effect which is not documented in any similar locale around the world—has led many investigators to float the possibility of paranormal forces at work there. Indeed, despite its picturesque location, the Overtoun Bridge does have something of a sinister history. Some unconfirmed historical research has floated the notion that this area may have been a centre for dark and violent pagan rituals among early Scotland's pre-Christian Celtic population. These reports, however, have not been confirmed.

One tragic incident that *has* been confirmed happened much more recently. In 1994, a mentally ill man named Kevin Moy murdered his infant son by throwing him off the bridge, then attempted suicide by cutting his wrists and jumping off the bridge himself (though he survived and was later committed to a mental asylum). Moy, who was later diagnosed with paranoid schizophrenia, was allegedly under the delusion that a birthmark on the boy's body was evidence that he was the devil incarnate. Moy possibly chose the Overtoun bridge as the location for the hideous act due to its reputation for potential "devil worship" in the earliest days of Scotland's history.

Some have speculated that the dogs who jump from the bridge are drawn by the restless spirit of Moy's slain infant, whose spectral cries may be audible to canine ears, if not human ones. However, as previously stated, the reports of dogs jumping from the bridge seem to go back all the way to the 1950s, and possibly even earlier, which would mean that this strange effect of the bridge began at least several decades before this particular tragedy occurred.

Despite these supernatural theories, other experts *have* attempted to produce more natural explanations for this bizarre phenomenon. One common thread in many of the accounts of dogs jumping from the bridge is that the incident occurs on a sunny and dry day. This has led some to speculate that either a scent or a high-pitched sound—or some combination of the two—that are most noticeable by dogs on clear days may be triggering this behaviour. One particular theory that has gained some traction notes that the wooded area on the banks around the bridge often houses numerous small mammals. For example, minks who live and mate in the area around the bridge would possibly produce a strong smell—one that, while imperceptible to humans, would be extremely powerful to a dog's superior olfactory senses—that would induce a dog's predatory instincts. And certainly, most dog owners can attest that even well-trained dogs can sometimes forget themselves when they encounter the sight or scent of a small mammal before them. Thus, it's not inconceivable that the sounds and smells of such creatures could be responsible for Overtoun Bridge's strange track record with canine visitors.

However, this theory does not quite explain why the "dog suicide" phenomenon is so prevalent as this one particular bridge, in a way that is not found in any other such area in the world. After all, minks and other small mammals certainly exist all over the planet, including in the areas around countless bridges where dogs walk every single day. And yet, while passing dogs may show some interest in a mink's scent or the scurrying body of a passing squirrel, none of these bridges have seen anything like the consistent phenomenon of "dog suicides" in the way that Overtoun Bridge has.

Another theory, albeit one that has not had much in terms of investigation, is that some specific but unknown quality of the bridge or the water below produces a highly unique sound that is particularly attractive to dogs. A dog's auditory range is capable of picking up sounds that are too high pitched to be consciously picked up by human ears. Thus, some have speculated that something in or around the bridge produces an extremely high-pitched sound that cannot be detected by humans but which serves as an otherwise inexplicable "siren call" for any dog passing by. However, as previously noted, no acoustic experiments are known to have been performed on the bridge to determine if this is the case. Additionally, experts are unclear what, if any, specific characteristics of the bridge or nearby burn would be producing such a sound in a way that would *not* be produced by any of the other countless similar bridges around the world.

Finally, one more contrived (but still interesting) theory posits a potential "psychic connection" between the dogs and their owners. Many dog-lovers have noted that their beloved canines sometimes seem to be "in tune" with their emotional or psychological state, oftentimes seeming to pick up when their owners are feeling agitated or fearful and responding with a similar change in mood. According to this theory, the Overtoun Bridge's reputation as a spot for dog suicide may serve as something of a self-fulfilling prophecy. Dog owners who are aware of the bridge's ghastly history with dogs may experience a great deal of trepidation when walking their own dogs over it. Their dogs, picking up on their owner's sudden surge in anxiety, may find themselves driven to act in a particular way that will lead them to attempt to jump from the bridge—the very outcome that their owners had feared in the first place.

Of course, this theory has more than a few holes. For one, it would be unclear why a sudden surge in anxiety picked up from their owners would make dogs *more* likely to abandon caution and jump carelessly over the side of the bridge. Additionally, there is the rather obvious point that dog owners who are already familiar with the bridge's reputation would probably not seek to walk their dogs over it in the first place.

It's also worth noting that, *despite* the bridge's unfortunate reputation, scores of town residents do, in fact, walk their dogs across the bridge every day, with little to no incident to show for it. Still, even if the so-called "dog suicides" are slightly blown out of proportion by a sensationalist media, enough cases have been documented to make for a legitimate and prolonged mystery and would probably render it wise for any animal lover walking their beloved dog through the streets of Dumbarton to reconsider their route if they seem themselves approaching a seemingly non-descript stone bridge overlooking a small ravine and mysterious, secret waterway.

Chapter 10
The Voynich Manuscript

Having explored macabre disappearances and mass dog deaths, we now thankfully turn to a mystery that is far less sinister, though no less intriguing. Among the extensive volumes of strange and fascinating books housed in the Beinecke Rare Book and Manuscript Library at Yale University is a particular item that has baffled scholars, scientists, and historians for over a century. The Voynich Manuscript, as it is currently known, appears, on the surface, to be little different from most medieval manuscripts found in similar collections around the world. At 240 pages, the manuscript contains a combination of written text and colourful illustrations common among such manuscripts from pre-modern Europe. However, a closer look reveals that the contents of this particular manuscript—both the text and the illustrations—are far stranger than anything else ever uncovered from that time period.

As per the time and place from which it supposedly originated, the Voynich Manuscript is classified as a medieval *codex*—a bound collection of sheets made from tanned animal skin (known as vellum) featuring written texts interspersed with illustrations and intricate diagrams. Subsequent radiocarbon dating done at the University of Arizona has indicated that the vellum in this particular manuscript was likely made in the early 15th Century, likely between 1404 and 1438. Additionally, experts believe that the specific animal skin from which the manuscript's vellum pages were made originated in Northern Italy.

So, why is it so mysterious? Well, for one, the script that is found throughout the entire book is not a language that has ever been seen by anyone. This is not to say that the writing is simple gibberish. Linguists and cryptographers have closely analysed the writing and found that it shares numerous characteristics with coherent writing in an actual grammatical language. Actual languages, when written out, tend to feature specific characters and character groupings that appear in regular intervals, corresponding to specific spelling conventions and morphological patterns in that language. The language found in the Voynich Manuscript *does* have these features, meaning that whoever wrote it was likely writing actual sentences in a coherent language, rather than just jotting down meaningless gibberish or random clusters of prewritten characters.

Despite this, however, the language itself—and even the script that it is written in—bear no clear resemblance to any language known by historians or linguists. While a few of the repeated characters do share some resemblance to recognizable characters from the Latin alphabet (such as characters that resemble an *O* or a lower-case *a*), many other characters do not correspond to any known written alphabet. As a result, the actual words and sentences themselves are completely indecipherable.

The manuscript's numerous illustrations are no less puzzling. While many of the illustrations found in medieval codex manuscripts *do* tend towards the bizarre, the Voynich Manuscript bears illustrations that are strange in very specific ways. Many of the illustrations portray detailed pictures of various plants, suggesting that these sections may have been meant to serve as some kind of botany guide. The issue is that many of the plants portrayed in the images do not seem to be any plant species recognized by botanists today, or at least not plants that would have existed in Europe in the Middle Ages.

Another section portrays astrological diagrams that seem to depict strange and unrecognizable constellations. While these diagrams *do* seem to portray some elements of traditional zodiac symbols—such as the *Pisces* fish and the *Taurus* bull—the portrayals of the sun, moon, and stars do not appear to conform to recognizable astronomical patterns, even taking into account the limited astronomical knowledge available to an educated person in the Middle Ages.

Other illustrations portray strange and mythical animals, including some figures that appear to resemble dragons. Many pages contain images of nude women, many of whom are portrayed as bathing in a wide variety of different kinds of pools and tubs. More strangely, many of these pools appear to be designed in the form of the female reproductive system. Still more pictures are abstract figures that are difficult to decipher in terms of what, if anything, they are supposed to represent.

Based on common themes in the images, scholars who have studied the manuscript have come up with a rough interpretation of how the book is organized. The first part contains the bulk of the images of plants and herbs, which, given how they are presented, would suggest that this section deals with pharmacology, a somewhat common theme among medieval manuscripts for the education of apothecaries. The next section likely portrays what are meant to be astrological charts, though the exact details of which constellations and astrological figures they are representing are unclear. The next section, the one containing the images of women bathing in strangely-shaped tubs and pools, is the least clear in terms of its meaning, but most scholars believe that this section is meant to expand upon the field of "balneology," or the study of baths and bathing, usually for the specific purpose of treating disease. The final section in the manuscript, as it exists today, contains fewer images but larger blocks of texts. Due to how the texts are arranged, scholars believe that this section may include recipes for either herbal drugs, alchemical potions, or simply various types of food and drink. Despite this rough outline, however, experts also believe that several pages of the original manuscript are missing, having been lost somewhere along the centuries, and thus that a definitive organization of the book's various sections may prove impossible with the book as it is.

So, given all of this, the obvious question is, therefore, where did this book come from? And in that regard, scholars *have* been able to determine some clear answers, albeit ones that have raised even further questions.

The manuscript first came into broad awareness in the early 20th Century, when it was purchased by its current namesake, Wilfrid Voynich. Voynich was a Polish-Lithuanian book dealer who specialized in rare and valuable manuscripts, particularly from medieval Europe. In 1912, heard of a possible sale of several antiquated medieval manuscripts by the Collegio Romano in Rome. The Collegio Romano, a Catholic Jesuit institution, was at the time suffering from financial hardships, and as a result, was considering selling a number of potentially valuable medieval manuscripts to the Vatican Library. Voynich, with his keen sense for business dealings, was able to swoop in during the sale and acquire many of these manuscripts for himself. Many of these volumes were indeed valuable but recognizable medieval codices, of the kind easily identified by any dedicated medievalist. But one...one was *different*.

While the manuscript that now bears Voynich's name had likely spent in excess of 200 years sitting forgotten in the back of the Collegio Romano library, Voynich himself recognized its potential value, not least of which because it seemed to have been written in a language neither he nor anyone he contacted had ever seen before. Following the purchase, Voynich and his wife moved to New York, and he spent the next several years engaged in two related—but potentially contradictory—activities. One, trying to find someone who could decipher the manuscript's strange text, and two, trying to sell it for an exorbitant price. While his failure to accomplish the former may have made the latter more likely, the manuscript remained unsold at the time of Voynich's death in 1930.

With Voynich now deceased, ownership of the manuscript passed to his wife, the British writer, and musician Ethel Lilian Boole Voynich. Ethel herself had a somewhat remarkable intellectual pedigree. The daughter of noted mathematician George Boole, Ethel achieved a significant degree of success and renown in the late 19th Century for her novels such as *The Gadfly*, as well as several musical pieces that she composed and performed (a rare feat for a woman at the time). Ethel also apparently excelled in longevity. While her husband died of cancer in 1930 at the age of 64, Ethel would outlive him by 30 years, dying in 1960 in her New York City apartment at the age of 96.

In her will, Ethel Voynich made reference to a particular manuscript that she had inherited from her late husband's extension collection, one which she specified must be given to the custody of her close friend Anne Nil, or else one of a select group of trustworthy scholars. This was, of course, the strange and indecipherable manuscript that her husband had sought to sell for a small fortune, though achieving no success. With Nil in possession of the book, she then managed to sell it to another interested book dealer named Hans P. Kraus. However, though clearly recognizing its value, Kraus, like Voynich, was unable to find a buyer willing to pay the substantial price he believed the manuscript to be worth. Thus, finally abandoning the pursuit of selling it at all, Kraus ultimately donated the book to Yale University in 1969. Today, the book is still on display at Yale's Beinecke Library, with all of its existing contents available online as well.

But the manuscript, by all appearances, was created long before 1912. So, where did it come from before Voynich purchased it from the Collegio Romano? That answer is much murkier, although, as of this writing, historians and other scholars who have studied the manuscript *have* compiled a rough timeline of who owned the book at what time. One of the biggest clues to this is a letter found tucked in the manuscript's margins. This letter, thankfully, is written in legible Latin rather than an indecipherable mystery language. Dated August 15, 1665 (or '66), the letter is from a man named Jan Marek Marci, a Bohemian physician, scholar, and then-rector of the University of

Prague. The letter is addressed to Athanasius Kircher, a Jesuit scholar, and polymath who, at the time, taught at the Collegio Romano. In the letter, Marci requests that Kircher examine the manuscript that he has sent him in hopes that Kircher would be able to make some sense out of it. The letter reads as follows:

> Reverend and Distinguished Sir, Father in Christ:
>
> This book, bequeathed to me by an intimate friend, I destined for you, my very dear Athanasius, as soon as it came into my possession, for I was convinced that it could be read by no one except yourself.
>
> The former owner of this book asked your opinion by letter, copying and sending you a portion of the book from which he believed you would be able to read the remainder, but he at that time refused to send the book itself. To its deciphering he devoted unflagging toil, as is apparent from attempts of his which I send you herewith, and he relinquished hope only with his life. But his toil was in vain, for such Sphinxes as these obey no one but their master, Kircher. Accept now this token, such as it is and long overdue though it be, of my affection for you, and burst through its bars, if there are any, with your wonted success.
>
> Dr. Raphael, a tutor in the Bohemian language to Ferdinand III, then King of Bohemia, told me the said book belonged to the Emperor Rudolph and that he presented to the bearer who brought him the book 600 ducats. He believed the author was Roger Bacon, the Englishman. On this point, I suspend judgment; it is your place to define for us what view we should take thereon, to whose favour

and kindness I unreservedly commit myself
and remain

At the command of your Reverence,
Joannes Marcus Marci of Cronland
Prague, 19th August, 1665 [or 1666]

This letter provides a few clues as to the manuscript's earlier history, both from the contents of the letter itself and from the identity of the person writing it. Marcie, a native of Bohemia (today the Czech Republic), identifies an "intimate friend" from whom he had gotten the manuscript. Today, scholars are fairly certain that this friend was Georg Baresch, a Bohemian alchemist and antique collector. In fact, scholars have turned up letters from Baresch himself to Kircher, asking for assistance in deciphering the manuscript as early as 1639. Baresch's attempt at correspondence, however, does not appear to have produced anything, possibly due to Baresch's potential reputation as being somewhat obnoxious and egotistical.

More intriguingly, however, is Marci's claim that the manuscript had once belonged to "Emperor Rudolf." This would have been Rudolf II, who ruled as Holy Roman Emperor from 1576 to 1612. And, to a certain extent, Rudolf II's association with the manuscript would make some degree of sense. Among other things, Rudolf II is primarily remembered today as a great patron of arts and literature, but also for a notable interest in the occult and in the burgeoning scientific understanding of the world (the line between these two areas was much more blurred in the late 16th Century than it is today). However, for many years following the discovery of this letter, scholars had little to no evidence specifically trying the manuscript to Rudolf II in any clear way.

That changed with a potentially ground-breaking discovery within the manuscript itself. On the manuscript's first page, nearly invisible to the naked eye was discovered the remnants of a signature. This signature was eventually identified as being that of Jakub Hořčický, also known as Jacobus Sinapius, a Bohemian apothecary of the early 17th Century who served as Rudolf II's personal physician and head of royal botanical gardens. This would lend credence to a popular theory that the Voynich Manuscript had at least an association with Rudolf II's royal court, if not with the Holy Roman Emperor himself.

If the manuscript *had* once been in the personal possession of Rudolf II, it likely would have passed over to Hořčický following the Emperor's death in 1612, possibly as a residual payment for Hořčický's services. The exact chain of events that led it to pass from Hořčický to Baresch to Marci is unclear, but as all three men lived in and around Prague in the early- to mid-17th Century, and as all had varying levels of ties to alchemical practices, literary interests, and other intellectual pursuits, the specific line of transfer is not hard to imagine.

Based on all of this information, scholars have created a crude but somewhat detailed chain of possession for the manuscript going back to the late 16th Century. Around the year 1600, the manuscript was in possession of Holy Roman Emperor Rudolf II—or at least his court in Prague—then to Hořčický, then to Baresch, then to Marci, who subsequently sent it to Rome in an attempt to see if Athanasius Kircher's expertise could shed some light on its puzzling contents. Kircher, apparently having no luck, relegated it to a back shelf in the Collegio Romano, where it sat for more than 200 years until acquired by Voynich in 1912.

However, here we hit a dead end. Recall that the vellum on which the manuscript is written was carbon-dated to the early 15th Century, likely sometime between 1404 and 1434. Rudolf II, however, was not born until 1552 and did not become Holy Roman Emperor until 1576. This leaves at least a century and a half between the manuscript's likely creation and its acquisition by Rudolf II's court. The mysteries of who created it, for what purpose, where it spent the first century and a half of its existence, and how exactly it found its way to Rudolf II's court in Prague all remain complete mysteries to this day.

Thus, with all definite or likely historical information dried up, we must now turn to the numerous theories and explanations from the ensuing years. The first of which was floated by Marci in his letter to Kircher. Marci had, in his letter, mentioned that a "Dr. Raphael" had believed that the manuscript was the creation of "Roger Bacon, the Englishman." This theory, on a rudimentary level, does make some degree of sense. Roger Bacon was a notable English scholastic philosopher and Franciscan friar of the High Middle Ages, who is best remembered today for his early contributions to the philosophy of empiricism and an early form of what would become the scientific method. Given Bacon's extensive writings, touching on areas such as alchemy, astrology, and pharmacology (all apparent subjects of the Voynich Manuscript, based on the illustrations at least), it is not out of the question that Bacon might produce something like the manuscript. Given his work on language and proto-versions of the field of linguistics, it is also not inconceivable that Bacon would develop his own constructed language with which to write, potentially keeping such closely guarded secrets indecipherable from potential enemies and plagiarists.

There is, alas, a rather significant problem with this hypothesis. Bacon died around the year 1292, at least a hundred years *before* when the Voynich Manuscript was carbon-dated to. Thus, most contemporary scholars feel fairly comfortable throwing this explanation out the window, however romantic or satisfying it may be (Dr. Raphael, of course, did not have the benefit of modern radiocarbon dating techniques, so contemporary investigators, in this case, should probably cut him a degree of slack for the error).

Outside of this erroneous reference to Roger Bacon, contemporary scholars have no real leads as to the manuscript's creation or location before the year 1600. Thus, in search of an explanation, some have turned to Rudolf II's court itself.

Many contemporary investigators have turned their attention to the possible involvement of two mysterious and intriguing figures associated with Rudolf II's court. John Dee and Edward Kelley, both natives of England, worked in various capacities as supposed mathematicians, apothecaries, and other more "legitimate" scientific fields. However, they have achieved renown—and a degree of infamy—for their association with alchemy and occultism. Dee himself had a degree of legitimacy for his track record as a royal astronomer for the court of England's Elizabeth I, but, through his association with Kelley, sold himself to the nobility of Europe as an expert in magical practices and the occult. Kelley, as his partner, claimed to have special powers as a spiritual medium, and the two of them would often sell their services to wealthy and powerful nobles throughout Europe as being able to contact the dead, conjure spirits, and engage in other esoteric occult practices.

Given Rudolf II's interest in occultism and alchemy, it's no surprise that Dee and Kelley found a warm welcome at his court—at least at first. Kelley, in particular, received a knighthood from the Holy Roman Emperor for his promise to produce gold from lead for the imperial court. However, Kelley's relationship with Emperor Rudolf soon soured—in 1591, Rudolf had Kelley arrested, ostensibly on the charge that he had killed another high-ranking courtier in a duel. However, some historians believe that Rudolf had grown sceptical of Kelley's alleged ability to turn lead into gold, given that none had been produced since Kelley's arrival in court, and the emperor wished to keep Kelley under wraps until this ability could be verified. Unfortunately for everyone involved, no gold would ever be produced, as Kelley would die in 1587 or 1598, allegedly in a fall during an attempt to escape from the tower in which he was imprisoned.

Despite this inauspicious end, there is no doubt that Dee and Kelley engaged in much supposedly occult work while employed at Rudolf II's court in the late 16th Century.

Whether one believes that the pair were mere con artists, generally believed themselves to have occult powers, or actually *did* possess such powers, it is not a stretch to believe that Dee and Kelley might be inclined to produce something like the Voynich Manuscript.

Though historians have thus far not been able to uncover direct evidence of Dee and Kelley's involvement in the manuscript, its contents do correspond to their common modus operandi. For example, much consternation has been dedicated to the strange, incomprehensible but seemingly coherent language of the manuscript's written text. In their supposed occult activities, Dee and Kelley claimed to be able to communicate with angels, with Kelley, in particular, going into an apparent trance and conversing with celestial beings in an angelic language he termed "Enochian." Dee would purport to provide dictation of these conversations. Thus, some who have investigated the case, both sceptic and believer, have floated the notion that the strange language found in the manuscript might be this very angelic language with which Kelley supposedly communicated with the Divine.

If this *were* a deliberate hoax on their part, Dee and Kelley would, of course, still need to dedicate an extraordinary number of hours and intellectual effort in producing the manuscript. Bear in mind, the language contained within is, by all appearances, a coherent, self-contained language with actual grammatical rules, consistent morphemes, and an extended vocabulary, rather than mere gibberish. Thus, Dee and Kelley would not only have needed to go through the extensive process of writing down hundreds of pages of nonsense text upon 200-year-old vellum while adding their own intricate illustrations—but they also would have needed to *construct* the language and its alphabet from scratch.

Of course, this effort, though highly labour intensive, may have ultimately been worth it. In his letter to Kircher, Marci mentioned that Emperor Rudolf had supposedly paid

"600 Ducats" for the manuscript, a substantial sum in those days. If Dee and Kelley were on the receiving end of that payment, then any effort they would have needed to expend to produce the fake manuscript would likely have been cost-effective (assuming, as many do, that the pair were only in it for the money).

Though the manuscript's actual vellum pages were dated to about 200 years before Dee and Kelley were working at Rudolf II's court, it would not have been inconceivable that the pair would have somehow been able to procure blank vellum pages from Northern Italy from about a century or two earlier, should they wish to present to the emperor a more seemingly "antiquated" codex volume.

However, this account remains entirely speculative, as no actual evidence has either directly or indirectly tied either Dee or Kelley to the manuscript's creation. The theory also does not provide much in terms of an explanation for the manuscript's illustrated contents. If Dee and Kelley had, in fact, created the manuscript as part of an elaborate con, why would they have included such a disproportionate number of illustrations of plants and herbs, as well as women in various stages of bathing?

One additional theory of the manuscript's authorship is that it was created by a 15th Century Italian engineer and polymath named Giovanni Fontana. This theory is based largely on circumstantial evidence. Unlike Bacon, who lived about 100 years before the time the manuscript was dated to, and unlike Dee and Kelley, who lived about 100 years *after*, Fontana did live in the early 15th Century, having died around the year 1455. This would place his life well within the timeframe where the manuscript's vellum pages were dated to. Additionally, Fontana was a native of the then city-state of Venice, placing his origin in the same region around Northern Italy where scholars believe the manuscript's vellum originated from.

Fontana was also noted for his detailed codices, often detailing medicinal, botanical, and engineering findings with added illustrations. Proponents of this theory noted that the illustrations in many of Fontana's manuscripts *do* somewhat resemble the style of the illustrations in the Voynich Manuscript. Finally, Fontana was known to employ cryptography to write his findings in coded language in order to disguise them from potential enemies. Though none of his extant writings specifically contain text that resembles the mysterious text of the Voynich Manuscript, the fact that Fontana would have been familiar with cryptography and constructed languages around the time of the manuscript's dating would at least suggest he could create such a secret language in the early 15th Century.

However, despite these circumstantial details, as of today, no further evidence of any kind has directly tied Fontana to the Voynich Manuscript, and any attempts to uncover such evidence, or to draw clear correspondences between the text and illustrations in Fontana's manuscripts with those in the Voynich, has so far proven either fruitless or so contrived as to warrant no further consideration.

More recently, several additional theories of the manuscript's contents have been proposed by academics, though none without considerable controversy.

The first in-depth attempt at deciphering the manuscript's unusual script was made in 1921 by University of Pennsylvania professor William Romaine Newbold. Newbold, rather than attempting to construe the manuscript's text as a coherent yet unknown language, produced an alternate interpretation based upon the process of "micrography," or the use of miniature letters used in intricate geometric patterns to produce coded or ulterior communication. According to Newbold's theory, the actual observable text found in the manuscript does not represent any actual meaning at all. However, Newbold conjectured that some minuscule markings found within a magnified viewing of individual letters *do* represent coherent linguistic markings. Newbold further theorized that these hidden letters might have been based on a shorthand script derived from ancient Greek.

Newbold further claimed that he was able to use this theory to translate entire paragraphs of the manuscript's texts into English, ostensibly producing coherent sections that detailed advanced knowledge of astronomy and chemistry unknown in the Middle Ages. However, most experts who have reviewed this theory have raised several significant issues with it. For one, the level of micrography needed to produce the hidden meaning that Newbold supposedly found was well beyond the capabilities of anyone in the 15th Century. Secondly, Newbold's argument also asserted that the text is based on findings from microscopes and telescopes that would have been far more advanced than anything available to even the wealthiest scholars at the time the manuscript was dated to. Additionally, many language and cryptographic experts have pointed out that Newbold's supposed "Greek shorthand" is extremely contrived and post hoc. In other words, Newbold appears to have concocted the theory first and then worked backward to force a coherent meaning upon random markings and scribbles found when looking at the manuscript's text under a microscope. In fact, later scholars have pointed out that Newbold's supposed means of assigning meaning to these markings were so open-ended that anyone intrepid enough could theoretically create any kind of meaning that he or she wanted, with about as much justification as Newbold's supposed "Greek shorthand." Thus, while Newbold's claim may have been initially taken seriously by some high-profile people (including Voynich himself), in the years since, most experts on the manuscript have completely dismissed it.

Another theory is far more recent. In 2017, Greg Kondrak, a linguistics professor at the University of Alberta, presented an intriguing explanation at that year's conference for the Association of Computational Linguistics. According to Kondrak's theory, the language in the manuscript is actually based on a form of medieval Hebrew, albeit a version written in an alphagram script. In other words, the letters of each word would have been rearranged alphabetically to obscure the text's meaning. Using this theory, Kondrak and his graduate students used an artificial intelligence program to translate a coherent meaning from the text. According to his report, the first sentence of the manuscript was translated as: "She made recommendations to the priest, man of the house and me and people."

This, though technically a grammatically correct English sentence, makes little to no rational sense. As a result, Kondrak's findings have been heavily disputed since he presented them. In fact, in Kondrak's own paper on the subject, he admitted that he and his team needed to make an abundance of "corrections" to the text as they found it in order to make it bear some degree of sense in Hebrew. Kondrak's theory, therefore, appears to fall into a similar problem to that of Newbold's: Kondrak developed a theory of interpretation *first* and then worked backward to force a predetermined meaning upon the text.

Kondrak's findings were also disputed by experts in the Hebrew language, who have pointed out numerous errors and liberties taken by Kondrak's team, even accepting the alphagram interpretation of what is supposed to be Hebrew script. Kondrak didn't exactly help his case when he admitted that he used Google Translate—not exactly a reputable academic source—as a means of translating information into Hebrew. Thus, while Kondrak and his team may have sparked renewed interest in the manuscript in recent years, their theory has yet to catch on among mainstream academia.

The third, most recent, theory was developed by Gerard Cheshire, a professor of biology at the University of Bristol, in 2019. Cheshire argued that the mysterious script found in the manuscript might actually be what he termed a "calligraphic Proto-Romance language," which he was able to decipher. Cheshire's theory is based upon the historical point that, up through the Middle Ages, most of the writing done in Europe was done in Latin and was written by a relatively small group of well-educated members of the clergy and nobility. The vast majority of "commoners" who spoke "vulgar" languages were not literate, and thus few of these languages were written down during the time that the Voynich Manuscript was supposedly written. Cheshire theorized that the strange script found in the manuscript may have been an attempt at transliterating a "Proto-Romance language," i.e., a vulgar language that served as a root language from which other languages in the Romance family—such as Italian, Spanish, French, etc.—all evolved from. Because few of the European non-Latin languages were written down, there were few attempts to transliterate them into the Latin alphabet, and so Cheshire believed that this manuscript may have been an attempt to create a new alphabet for a Proto-Romance language before such languages were more commonly codified in the Latin alphabet.

Even more boldly, Cheshire claimed to have translated large portions of the text based upon what he called "lateral thinking and ingenuity." According to his account, the manuscript mainly contains advice for women, touching on subjects such as helpful medicinal plants, bathing practices, parenting skills, and relevant astrological readings. Cheshire further theorized that the manuscript was produced by Dominican nuns for a female royal. Here, he specifically mentions Maria of Castile, the Queen consort of Aragon from 1416 to 1458.

However, as with the other theories mentioned here, Cheshire's proposal has been met with extensive skepticism and incredulity from other academics. Again, the core argument against Cheshire's theory is that he merely worked backward from a predetermined vantage point and concocted meaning from the text based upon what he wanted to read, not what the text actually said. Medieval Academy of America Executive Director Lisa Fagin Davis went so far as to call Cheshire's theory "just more aspiration, circular, self-fulfilling nonsense." The University of Bristol,

Cheshire's own institution, also distanced themselves somewhat from this theory, releasing a statement reinforcing that the research "was entirely [Cheshire's] own work and is not affiliated with the University of Bristol, the School of Arts nor the Centre for Medieval Studies."

Of course, as with all things of this nature, there are several more "far-fetched" theories as well. The most notable of these holds that the manuscript is, in fact, not of Earthly origins at all, but rather the product of alien intelligence. Proponents of this theory believe that the mysterious, indecipherable language found within the manuscript is not a *human* language at all, but rather the language used by whichever race of extra-terrestrials supposedly visited our planet in the early 15th Century. In terms of "evidence," this theory *would* explain the strange and seemingly advanced astrological illustrations found in the manuscript, which (possibly) show constellations and star formations that would have been beyond the knowledge of anyone living around the year 1400. This could also explain how the manuscript was able to include detailed images of strange plants, some of which may have only been found in parts of the world inaccessible to medieval Europeans. Of course, this theory also raises even more questions, such as why an alien race that is supposedly advanced enough to travel lightyears through space to visit Earth would employ a method as primitive as hand-written text on vellum as their preferred means of record-keeping.

So, is the manuscript an esoteric occult manual? A record of a now-dead language? A work of extra-terrestrials? An elaborate hoax? It is possible that someday a code-breaker or linguist will finally crack the mystifying text that has baffled their predecessors for centuries. It's also possible that a new historical finding will shed more light on the manuscript's origins or journeys before it comes into our historical picture around the year 1600. But, until then, the Voynich Manuscript will remain an intriguing and engaging curiosity, standing out among the countless volumes of rare and valuable books in the distinguished halls of Yale

University, waiting for someone to finally come along and reveal its secrets.

Chapter 11
The Mystifying Case of the Black Dahlia

The haunting murder of Elizabeth Short has become firmly entrenched in our collective imaginations almost eighty years since it took place. This lasting impact of a single murder of a single young woman stems from a number of factors that all converge in a single act of violence: Short's beautiful and haunting *femme fatale* aesthetic, her tragic backstory, a backdrop of the ostensibly gilded world of Hollywood, and the unspeakably gruesome nature of the crime itself. But, of course, arguably the most memorable element of this case comes not from the details of the crime or the setting, but rather from the dark, haunting pseudonym with which Short has come to be known in the years following her death. Though born Elizabeth Short, she would posthumously become known around the world as simply "the Black Dahlia."

On January 15, 1947, at around 10 AM, Betty Bersinger was walking down South Norton Avenue in the Leimert Park neighbourhood of Los Angeles. On her way to visit a shoe repair shop, Bersinger had brought along her three-year-old daughter for what she assumed would be a rather uneventful morning errand routine. At the time, Leimert Park was not as well developed as other areas of the city, and so the surrounding blocks were often adorned by vacant lots and underdeveloped plots of land. These lots, as one would imagine, rarely drew much interest from passers-by. However, as she and her daughter walked down the block between Coliseum Street and West 39th Street, something in one of the lots drew Bersinger's attention.

According to her later recounting, she, at first, thought the pale and humanoid form that she caught out of the corner of her eye—lying in a strange position in one of the empty lots—was nothing more than a discarded department store mannequin. The figure was so pale and lifeless that Bersinger initially could not imagine it to be anything other than a plastic or wax figure, probably discarded by a lazy store employee looking to save some time on the way to the landfill.

But, at the same time, another, more prescient part of Bersinger's psyche whispered that...*something* was amiss in the situation. Maybe it was the strangely human-like black hair that Bersinger caught upon the body's head from the surrounding grasses. Maybe it was the somewhat strange and almost deliberate sprawl of the body's limbs. Maybe it was just a general sense of unease in the otherwise deserted location. Whatever the reason, Bersinger decided to venture over for a closer look. What she found there would come to haunt both her and the entire city of Los Angeles for the foreseeable future.

As she grew closer to the figure, Bersinger realized with mounting horror that it was *not,* in fact, a mere mannequin or wax figure carelessly dumped in an empty lot. It was, by all appearance, a *body*. As if the discovery of an actual dead body were not horrible enough, the state that the body was in would be more than enough to infest one's nightmares for the rest of their life.

The body had once been a young woman, possibly no older than her early twenties as far as could be ascertained from the corpse. As Bersinger had earlier noticed, the woman's hair was coloured a thick, jet black. The blackness of the woman's hair, however, contrasted sharply with the coloration of the rest of her body. As Bersinger herself later noted: "I glanced to my right, and saw this very dead, white body...my goodness, it was so white. It didn't...look like anything more than perhaps an artificial model. It was so white...."

The woman was naked, lying on her back with her face up and her arms and legs sprawled out from her body, almost as if they had been posed at deliberate angles. Both corners of her mouth had been mutilated, her killer having carved a grotesque exaggerated "smile" into her cheeks, a type of mutilation commonly known as a "Glasgow smile." But, the most prevalent—and horrifying—detail was the one that would make this case stand out from all of the other anonymous and brutal murders that took place in Los Angeles in any given year—the woman's body had been cut completely in half.

 This bisection specifically occurred at the waist, her killer having cut through her lower torso width-wise, cleanly severing her abdomen and her second and third lumbar vertebrae. Both newly separated sections of her body were then displayed as they would have been on an intact body, only separated by about a foot. Many of the woman's internal organs, such as her intestines, had been gathered and neatly tucked underneath her buttocks.

 Shielding her daughter's eyes from the horrifying scene, Bersinger ran to the nearest occupied home and immediately phoned the authorities. As the first wave of police began to arrive at the scene, a large crowd of journalists and rubberneckers also began to accumulate. Among this group was journalist Aggie Underwood of the *Los Angeles Herald-Express*, notable as one of the first female journalists to serve as an editor of a major metropolitan newspaper. As police found themselves having to deal with the growing crowd rather than investigate the actual crime scene, Underwood managed to capture several photographs of the body as it was discovered. These photographs remain among the most famous of the case, although their grisly contents proved less than suitable for the weak of stomach.

 When detectives were finally able to more properly investigate the crime scene itself, they made a few additional grisly discoveries. For one, the reason for the body's unnaturally white pallor soon became clear—it had been drained almost entirely of blood. Curiously, no blood lay under the body where it lay in the vacant lot. This detail suggested to detectives that it had been bisected somewhere else, and its subsequent pieces were brought to that location to be posed in some macabre display. Frustratingly, the body also appeared to have been washed, most likely, as police surmised, an attempt by the killer to remove any potential clues or identifying traces. Despite this, police did soon discover what, initially, looked like promising clues. In the vacant lot itself, police found a single heel print from a shoe, as well as tire tracks left in the dirt. Nearby, police also found a cement sack that contained traces of human blood and water.

Following the initial investigation, police attempted to transport the remains to the coroner's office while the press raced to get the gruesome story out as quickly as possible. Of course, save for the basic facts of a bisected and mutilated woman's body found in an empty lot, no one at this point knew much of anything, including the woman's identity. That, of course, did not stop the L.A. newspapers, especially the *Los Angeles Examiner*, owned by notable (and infamous) media magnate William Randolph Hearst. Within days the story was being front-page news all across Los Angeles, with few graphic details spared (at least as far as 1940s standards would allow) and speculation and straight-up fiction filling the holes left in the absence of facts.

Frederick Newbarr, the Los Angeles coroner, eventually performed an autopsy on the body on January 16, the day after its discovery. Here, he uncovered a few other unsettling details—the victim bore ligature marks on her hands and feet, suggesting that she had been bound and likely abused over a period of time, in addition to ligature marks around her neck. She also had suffered severe blunt force trauma to her skull, likely resulting in a severe concussion. The victim also bore mutilation markings and tissue loss on her breasts, and trauma to her genitals and pelvic region suggested that she had been sexually assaulted. However, in examining the specific characteristics of her wounds and lacerations, Newbarr noted something else of potential relevance. The technique by which the body had been cut in half, rather than having been done as a crude and messy mutilation, appeared to show a rather high degree of surgical skill and precision. The incisions through her abdomen and spinal column corresponded to a specific surgical technique called a "hemicorporectomy," a very rare and very difficult surgical procedure in which the entire lower half of a person's body—in addition to internal organs of the lower abdomen—are removed. As this procedure was (and still is) performed quite rarely, and only in extreme circumstances where no other options may be of use to potentially save a life, a person with the anatomical and medical knowledge to perform such a procedure competently would have to have had a good deal of medical or surgical training. Eventually, Newbarr gave a cause of death as internal hemorrhaging brought on by extensive blows to the head and other physical trauma.

Following his lengthy enumeration of the violence brought upon the young woman's body, Newbarr went on to note some physical details of the woman herself. He noted that she was around 5 feet, 5 inches (or about 1.65 meters) tall and weighed 115 pounds. She also had blue eyes and brown hair, though the latter had been dyed a dark black. He also noted that her teeth were "badly decayed." More importantly, Newbarr was able to get usable fingerprints from the body, which were quickly sent to the FBI for potential identification.

Though Los Angeles, then as today, was no stranger to murders and violent crime, the specific level of violence presented in this case—not merely the savagery of the violence itself but also the graphic public display in which the body had been left—brought on an immediate level of media interest. Within a day of the story breaking, the main goal for both police and reporters was to identify the unfortunate woman to whom the mutilated corpse belonged. Fortunately, this proved to be a fairly simple question to answer. The FBI was, in fact, able to find a match on the fingerprints taken from the corpse, identifying them as belonging to a young woman by the name of Elizabeth Short. Short's fingerprints were on file from an earlier arrest for underage drinking in 1943, and shortly after the official announcement of her identity, the media—already well into a feeding frenzy—jumped into a battle to acquire the most detailed and gratuitous information about the unfortunate young woman, no matter what the means.

The most egregious and repulsive example of this came from William Randolph Hearst's *Los Angeles Examiner.* By using less than ethical means, the Examiner's reporters were able to obtain the phone number of Phoebe Short, mother of the recently-slain Elizabeth. Within a day of the release of Short's name, Examiner reporters were already calling the bereaved Mrs. Short for details of her late daughter's life. This would be fairly grotesque if Mrs. Short had, in fact, already been in mourning for her murdered daughter. However, the situation was made far worse by the fact that the Short family—including Mrs. Short herself—had not even yet been notified that their daughter had been murdered. Upon contacting Mrs. Short, the Examiner reporters got around this minor detail by simply lying and telling Mrs. Short that Elizabeth had, in fact, recently won a beauty contest in order to pry her for extensive personal information. Only after getting their fill of personal details of the late young woman did the reporters finally inform Mrs. Short of the horrible truth of what had happened to her daughter.

It was during the first week or so of frenzied media reports on the grisly case that Short was first given the moniker "the Black Dahlia," the term by which she quickly came to be identified. No one today quite understands the origin of the name. Some reports have suggested that this was, in fact, a nickname that Short had been given in life, possibly derived from her penchant for dressing in black dresses and dying her hair black. This, however, has never actually been confirmed, nor is it clear, if true, how the name made its way to the press. Another, more likely, scenario is that the name was derived from the 1946 film noir movie *The Blue Dahlia*, a somewhat popular movie at the time that corresponded both to the late Short's identification with the colour black and the press's habit at the time of giving memorable pseudonyms to victims of particularly newsworthy or scandalous crimes. Regardless of its origins, the name stuck, and even as the people in Los Angeles were following developments of the horrifying story, most came to know that victim not by her actual name but by this striking and tragic identifier.

But even as her actual name was obscured by what was either a friendly nickname or a press invention, the details of Short's life were soon being mined for any particularly relevant or interesting details. As per the normal operating procedures of a media frenzy, much of this information was exaggerated, embellished, or outright fabricated by a press more concerned with topping their competitors in the L.A. market than accurately informing their readers—or showing any kind of respect to the deceased. Even today, accurate biographical details about Short's life can sometimes be hard to fully separate from stories that the contemporary media either embellished or made up. For example, a common trope that is often repeated when discussing this case is that Short was an "aspiring actress." And while it's entirely possible that Short, like so many countless young women since the inception of the city's film industry, had moved to Los Angeles in the hopes of breaking into Hollywood, as of today, there is no evidence that Short ever had any acting credits to her name. Some less polished speculation goes in the other direction, pondering that Short, desperate in the face of a failed acting career, was forced to turn to high-end prostitution. This assertion also has no evidence supporting it from any of the information that has been uncovered about Short's life.

Here, then, is what *is* known about the woman herself. Elizabeth Short was born in Boston on July 29, 1924. Short was the middle daughter of five, born to father Cleo and mother, Phoebe Short. After a few moves around New England during her first few years, the then-three-year-old Short and her family settled in the Medford suburb of Boston in 1927, where she would remain for most of the rest of her childhood. The Short family life seemed, initially, to be somewhat comfortable, if not entirely prosperous. Cleo, the family patriarch, spent the 1920 working as a developer of miniature golf courses, a fairly popular pastime of the period, and a business that seemed as if it would keep the family finances stable. This, however, came crashing down in 1929, following that year's infamous stock market crash and the beginning of the Great Depression. Now financially ruined and facing bankruptcy, Cleo fled from his family in 1930. After his car was found empty and abandoned on a bridge overlooking Boston's Charles River, the Short family came to believe that he had committed suicide. Following this sudden trauma, Phoebe Short moved with her five daughters into a smaller Medford apartment, taking a job as a bookkeeper as a means of supporting her family.

Young Elizabeth was plagued with a series of health issues during her adolescence, including chronic bronchitis and asthma. These issues got so bad that she required an operation on her lungs when she was 15. Following this procedure, her doctors advised her to relocate to a warmer climate during the winter in order to inflict less cold-induced stress upon her respiratory system. Thus, Short spent the next three years living in Florida during the winter months, returning to her native Boston in the summer.

Then, in 1942, the family received what must have been something of a shock. A letter from Cleo Short himself, supposedly long dead by suicide, arrived one day in the mail, addressed to Phoebe Short and bearing a return address in California. In the letter, Cleo confessed that he was, in fact, very much alive. The stress and shame of the financial problems he had inflicted upon his family led him to fake his suicide and flee out west to start a new life. Now deeply apologetic and seeking reconciliation, Cleo inquired if Phoebe or any of his daughters might care to visit him in his new home in Vallejo, California. Phoebe herself, perhaps unsurprisingly, was not particularly keen on taking up this offer, but the now-18-year-old Elizabeth was. That year,

Elizabeth moved out west to stay with her estranged father in his home in Vallejo.

Unfortunately, whatever happy reunion the two shared did not last long. After a period of increasing tensions and fights between father and daughter, Short moved out of her father's house and began a brief period of indeterminate living, moving between locations in California and eventually ending up in San Diego. It was during this time that Short attained her underage drinking arrest that would later lead to her posthumous identification. Following her travels around California, Short returned to Florida, where she met an Army Air Force pilot named Matthew Michael Gordon Jr. The two began dating, though Gordon was scheduled to depart for service in the then-still ongoing World War II. Via letters sent between the two, Short accepted Gordon's proposal of marriage, to be made official upon his return from active duty. However, these plans would tragically be cut short when Gordon was killed in a plane crash in August of 1945, only a few weeks short of the war's official end.

Following her fiancé's death, Short returned to California, this time settling in Los Angeles in the summer of 1946. It was here that Short would spend most of the last few months of her life, mostly working as a waitress and potentially pursuing acting roles, though none ever came her way.

By January of 1947, Short had begun an affair with a married, 25-year-old salesman named Robert "Red" Manley. On the 9th of January, Short and Manley visited San Diego together, after which Manley dropped Short off at the downtown L.A.'s Biltmore Hotel, where she was allegedly staying. Short had told him that she was going to see her sister, who was visiting L.A. from Boston. Manley's account remains the last verified sighting of her alive. Some witnesses did later report that they saw Short using a phone booth in the hotel's lobby, and a few others reported seeing her on the evening of the 9th at the Crown Grill Cocktail Longue down the street from the Biltmore Hotel. If these reports are indeed accurate, they appear to be the last time anyone—other than her killer—saw Elizabeth Short alive. Following the night of the 9th, Short would not be seen again until her lifeless, naked, and the bisected body was found lying in a vacant lot on the morning of January 15.

As more and more details of the horrifying crime came to light, people around Los Angeles and the country as a whole began to ask variations of the same question: what kind of person could *do* something like this? But, as it turned out, the killer wouldn't be silent for too long. Within a week of the discovery of Short's body, a person (or persons) claiming to be the killer made contact with the media. Much like the earlier case of Jack the Ripper, these correspondences, whether legitimate or an elaborate hoax, took the form of a taunting brag, offering tantalizing details while mocking the investigation and promising more contact in the future. On January 21, six days after Short's body was discovered, Los Angeles Examiner editor James Richardson was called directly by a strange man who claimed that he was Short's killer. According to Richardson's account, the person on the other end of the line offered faux congratulations on his newspaper's coverage of the case and claimed that he would eventually turn himself in, though not before letting the cat and mouse game with police continue for a bit longer. Richardson also noted that the caller promised that he would send Richardson "some souvenirs of Beth Short in the mail."

Sure enough, a few days later, on January 24, the U.S. Postal Service in Los Angeles intercepted a suspicious manila envelope that was addressed to "The Los Angeles Examiner and other Los Angeles papers." The letter found inside was constructed from individual characters cut out of magazines, reading: "Here is Dahlia's belongings, letter to follow." Also included in the envelope were various items belonging to Short, including her birth certificate, photographs, written letters, and a datebook monogrammed with the name *Mark Hansen* and with several pages torn out. Despite attempts by the police and FBI to search the envelope for potential clues, they quickly found that the sender washed it and its contents in gasoline, destroying any potential fingerprints or other identifying evidence.

A few days later, on January 26, the Los Angeles Examiner received another letter from the supposed killer. This letter, unlike the previous one, was handwritten and read: "Here it is. Turning in Wed., Jan. 29, 10 am. Had my fun at police." The letter was signed *Black Dahlia Avenger*. This letter allegedly provided a specific location at which the sender claimed he would surrender to the police on the given date. However, though police swarmed the area on the morning of January 29, no killer arrived to turn himself in. Instead, the Examiner received more letters, once more comprised of cut-and-pasted magazine letters rather than handwriting, which said, among other things: "Have changed my mind. You would not give me a square deal. Dahlia killing was justified." These letters were also washed in gasoline, providing no meaningful clues or leads for investigators.

Less than a month into the case, a potential development came in the form of another grisly murder. On February 10, the body of 44-year-old Jeanne French was found in Los Angeles's Grand View Boulevard. Jeanne, like Short, was found naked and badly beaten, though she was not dismembered as Short had been. Of greater relevance, though, was the fact that her killer—or someone associated with her killing—had left a note on her stomach in lipstick, writing "Fuck you B.D.," and "Tex." When this was reported to the press, journalists made the obvious connection between the initials "B.D." and "Black Dahlia" and immediately framed this as the same deranged killer—often stylized as a "werewolf"—striking again. However, the lipstick message was somewhat smudged when it was found, and later analysis suggests that it actually read *P.D.* rather than *B.D.* If this were the case, the "P.D." would possibly refer to the police themselves rather than reference a previous crime. Unfortunately, French's murder, like Short's, has never been solved, and any potential connection between the two crimes remains unverified.

Despite the horrifying aspects of the crime and the widespread, sensationalized news coverage within the initial few weeks, the case eventually went cold. Supposed "clues" continued to appear but were either useless or dismissed as fraudulent. A few people attempt to "turn themselves in" for the crime, but are quickly determined to be mere cranks or attention-hungry outcasts. After a while, the press moved on from the Black Dahlia case, finding among the bleak and frenzied underbelly of Los Angeles an ample supply of new and juicy stories with which to draw readers' attention.

In the decades that followed Short's horrifying murder, dozens—or perhaps even hundreds—of potential suspects have been floated by professional and amateur investigators. Of these, only a few are given any credibility by relevant authorities, though no definitive evidence has ever been uncovered that would suffice for actual criminal charges. Some of these theories attempt to tie the Black Dahlia murder to other similar unsolved crimes. For example, one theory floats the notion that the Black Dahlia murder was also responsible for the Cleveland Torso murders from a decade prior. The Cleveland Torso Murderer, if you recall, was also notable for dismembering and mutilating his victims with surgical precision, though, aside from this superficial similarity in method, no other specific evidence has ever been uncovered linking the two killers (some speculation has later come out, offered by Eliot Ness's biographer, that Ness believed he knew the identity of both the Cleveland Torso Killer *and* the Black Dahlia murderer, though it is unclear how credible this belief was, or if Ness believed that the two killers were one and the same person).

Another theory links the Black Dahlia murder to a Chicago-area serial killer known as the "Lipstick Killer," who murdered three women and girls in the area around Chicago in 1945 and 1946, sometimes leaving notes written in lipstick at the scene of the crime. In fact, an LAPD Captain stated that he believed the crimes were related, though taking place in different cities. However, a man named William Heirens was arrested for the murders in 1946, a year before Short's murder, and was incarcerated at the time. Many have cast doubt on Heirens's guilt, however, given evidence that his confession was beaten out of him by police. Thus, room still exists that the Black Dahlia killer and the Lipstick Killer could be one and the same, though the theory is somewhat flimsy.

    Aside from this wanton speculation, a rather small number of potential suspects have come to receive the majority of attention from serious investigators on this case, though issues remain regarding each. One of the first major suspects, and perhaps the most obvious one given the background information of Short's life, is none other than Robert "Red" Manley himself. After all, Short and Manley were in something of a relationship at the time of her murder, and Manley was the last person known definitively to have seen Short alive. Evidence also came out that Manley had actually been discharged from the U.S. Army for supposed mental instability. In fact, a few years after Short's murder, Manley was committed to a mental asylum by his wife, on the grounds that he was suffering a mental breakdown and apparently "hearing voices." One additional suspicious detail from several decades later arose at Manley's death. On January 16, 1986, one day after the anniversary of the discovery of Short's body, Manley died following a fall in his home. The convenient timing of his death has raised a few more suspicions upon him as a potential suspect. However, though he was the top suspect by police at the start of the investigation, the LAPD was never able to find any actual evidence connecting him to the crime. In the days following Short's murder, Manley was able to pass two polygraph tests (though, recall that these are not exactly entirely reliable) and apparently had a verifiable alibi for the days in which Short would have been abducted and murdered. Thus, he was never arrested or charged with any crime in relation to Short's death, and today most case experts dismiss him as a suspect.

Another notable suspect is Mark Hansen. Recall that the datebook found within the letter sent to the Los Angeles Examiner—contained among various other items belonging to Short—was monogrammed as belonging to a "Mark Hansen." Hansen, as it turned out, was Short's landlord for a time when she was living in Los Angeles, and in fact, owned a nightclub where Short may have spent much of her time. Police also determined that Short had spoken to Hansen on the phone from San Diego a few days before her murder. In light of these facts, Hansen was brought in for questioning by the LAPD. However, as with Manley, police were unable to determine any specific evidence linking him to the crime. In terms of the datebook, though it belonged to him, he claimed that he never used it, and that Short must have taken it as her own when she was living as one of his tenants on his property. Some reports later indicated that Hansen may have tried to make a romantic pass at Short but was rejected. Other reports indicate that Hansen may have had connections to the LAPD, which supposedly may have helped him escape justice in this case. However, these charges are purely speculative, and to this date, nothing definitive has ever come out indicating that Hansen killed Short.

Other major suspects have been proposed, each offering both tantalizing circumstantial evidence but also some glaring issues. There is, for example, the case of Leslie Dillon, a 27-year-old bellhop and former mortician's assistant who had shown a sinister interest in sexual violence and sadism to LAPD detectives. There is also Patrick O'Reilly, a surgeon who likely knew Short from parties as Hansen's nightclub and who had previously been arrested for a violent sexual assault of his secretary, part of a broader pattern of engagement in sexual violence against women from his life. Additionally, there's the case of Walter Bayley, another surgeon who lived only a block away from where Short's body was found and whose daughter was a friend of Short's sister. Finally, there's the mysterious case of George Knowlton, about whom little is known directly, but whose daughter came forward in the 1990s reporting that she had—through therapy—recovered a suppressed memory of her father murdering and dismembering Elizabeth Short in the family kitchen when she was a child. Despite various degrees of promising leads associated with each of these suspects, ultimately, nothing became of any of them.

But today, by far, the best-known and most intriguing suspect in the case is George Hodel. Recent reviews of the documents from the initial investigation have revealed that Hodel was, in fact, considered a suspect by police early on, though not the *main* suspect, and not prominent enough to warrant any degree of media attention. In fact, it wasn't until 2003 that Hodel became intimately associated with the murder case long gone cold. This year saw the publication of *The Black Dahlia Avenger*, a detailed investigation of the case that eventually came to the conclusion that Hodel was, in fact, the murderer. What distinguished this book from any of the other countless volumes written about the case was who wrote it. The book's author was, as it so happened, a former LAPD detective named Steve Hodel, who also happened to be George Hodel's own son.

Hodel certainly fit the general profile of the Black Dahlia killer. He was a respected physician, and, though he worked primarily as a venereal disease specialist, he would have had the surgical knowledge to perform the precise dismemberments and mutilations of Short's body. Hodel, however, was also not a stranger to charges of sexual and physical violence. In 1948, a year after Short's murder, Hodel was arrested for allegedly sexually assaulting his own teenage daughter, Tamar. Despite these charges, Hodel was ultimately acquitted after several family members testified in his defence. However, in 1950 police still considered Hodel to be a major suspect in the Black Dahlia case, so much so that they were able to get legal authorization to place wiretaps in his home. During these recordings, Hodel was allegedly heard to say something to the effect of:

> Supposin' I did kill the Black Dahlia. They couldn't prove it now. They can't talk to my secretary anymore because she's dead.... They

thought there was something fishy. Anyway,
now they may have figured it out. Killed her.
Maybe I did kill my secretary....

The reference to the "secretary" was likely regarding the case of Ruth Spaulding, a former secretary of Hodel's who had died of a drug overdose in 1945. Police believed that it could actually have been murder. Hodel was considered the prime suspect, given that he delayed contacting authorities after discovering her body and had even burned some of her papers immediately afterward. Still, no charges were ever brought against Hodel due to lack of evidence, though the investigation into him persisted over the next few years.

In his 2003 book, Steve Hodel references these facts in building the case against his father. However, the real strength of his account lay in several new details that he was able to bring to light, given his close familial connection to the suspect. For example, Steve Hodel noted that the handwriting from the one handwritten letter sent to the press *did* closely match that of his father. He even hired a handwriting expert to compare the letter against samples of George Hodel's handwriting, who eventually determined a "close match," though not a *definite* match, between the two. Additionally, Steve Hodel found several previously unknown photographs in his father's records that showed a young woman who looked remarkably like Elizabeth Short. Though no evidence had made itself known that specifically indicates that Hodel knew Short when she was alive, Steve Hodel has argued that these photographs indicate some kind of close relationship between the two. The fact that George Hodel worked at a venereal disease clinic has raised speculation that Short may have needed to use his services surreptitiously, following from the theory that she had been working as a prostitute. This, however, has not been proven. In terms of the photographs themselves, Steve Hodel also hired facial recognition experts to compare the face of the woman in the photos to pictures of Short. These experts did conclude that, based upon their facial analysis, there was a "strong likelihood" that Elizabeth Short and the woman in Hodel's photos were one and the same. However, it must be stated that other independent facial recognition analysts not associated with Steve Hodel's investigation have remained sceptical of this claim, arriving at the conclusion that the two women were likely different people. And so, the matter of the identity of the woman in these pictures remains unresolved to this day.

Steve Hodel was able to present additional evidence of his father's guilt, though this remains more circumstantial than anything. For example, George Hodel was a noted aficionado of celebrity and the arts, often throwing parties for notable artists at his Los Angeles home. One artist with whom Hodel was apparently somewhat close was the surrealist artist Man Ray. Steve Hodel and other proponents of this theory have noted that the specific way in which Elizabeth Short's body was posed in the spot where it was left—limbs extend and arms left above her head with elbows bent—closely resembles the pose of a body featured in a 1933 Man Ray work known as *Minotaur*. Thus, the speculation goes that Hodel was attempting to use Short's mutilated body as a kind of "art," as if his deranged mind saw himself as trying to match the work of his artistic friend and rival.

Another intriguing—but undetermined—piece of evidence comes from George Hodel's later activities over the course of the next few decades. Perhaps fearing further prosecution for potential criminal activities, Hodel moved from the United States to the Philippines in 1950, remaining there for the next four decades until his return stateside in 1990. During the 40 years in which his father was a resident of the Philippines, Steve Hodel claims he has found examples of several unsolved murders of women that, according to him, seem to fit a similar profile to the Black Dahlia murder. In one particular case, Steve Hodel says he found a case in which the body of a missing Filipino woman was found mutilated and cut in half in much the same way the Elizabeth Short was. What's more, Steve Hodel argues that not only did this case coincide with the time in which his father was living in the Philippines, but it apparently occurred in close proximity to the specific area where George Hodel resided. This specific case, however, has not been definitively verified by other independent investigators, so most case experts outside of Steve Hodel's sphere have emphasized caution when dealing with suppositions involving George Hodel and the Philippines.

Steve Hodel's case certainly renewed interest in the Black Dahlia murder as a whole and *did* manage to win over a few notable people. Most prominently, former Los Angeles Deputy District Attorney Stephen Kay has been quoted as saying that he found Hodel's case against his father highly convincing and that "I would have no reservations about filing...counts of murder against Dr. George Hodel," based upon the evidence that Steve Hodel has presented. However, one should note that Kay had already retired from the Los Angeles County District Attorney's Office when he made that statement and was merely speaking on behalf of himself, rather than the actual D.A. department. As of today, the LAPD and the Los Angeles district attorney still consider this case technically "open," albeit long since gone inactive.

Today, cold case investigators and true crime enthusiasts consider the most frustrating aspect of the case to be the fact that a somewhat suspicious number of the original LAPD case files and collected evidence have seemingly gone missing in official records. The exact cause of this is unknown. Some have alleged an official coverup of some kind on the part of the police, perhaps lending credence to the theory that the killer was, in fact, someone with connections to powerful people. Others have ascribed this to mere incompetence on the part of the police, as the LAPD did not have the best reputation as an investigative or crime-fighting body during this time. Whatever the case, the lack of preserved evidence continues to frustrate would-be investigators today and casts a dark cloud of pessimism on any hope that the case might one day be solved.

Regardless of the merits of any of this supposition, one point has become painfully apparent with each passing year. Regardless of what new clues may yet be uncovered or what new theories may be floated, the hope of Elizabeth's Short's murderer being brought to justice has long since vanished. The initial clues found near her body—the tire tracks and bloody cement bags—may have seemed initially like promising leads but ultimately led detectives nowhere. In 2003, Ralph Asdel, the last of the case's original detectives still alive, stated in a *Los Angeles Times* interview that he believed he had in fact not only identified Short's killer, but *interviewed* him. This man was, he claimed, the occupant of the car seen parked near to where Short's body was found in its post-mortem state on the morning of January 15. However, he never stated who this suspect was or why he was never able to build a solid case against him, and thus whatever promising door that lead may have opened has long since closed.

With regards to the man whom many now regard as the most promising suspect, George Hodel lived in the Philippines until 1990, when he moved back to Los Angeles. Here, he lived out the remaining years of his life in relative anonymity, dying in 1999 at the age of 91. If he *was,* in fact, the man responsible for the sadistic murder of Elizabeth Short, as his son now believes, he had given authorities a good half-century to make their case against him. A half-century that, as it did with any other suspect, lead, or theory, produced nothing but smoke, mirrors, and whispers of something darker lurking beneath the shiny but gilded lights of Los Angeles.

Chapter 12
The Cleveland Torso Murderer

Just south of Lake Erie's southernmost shoreline, the Cuyahoga River twists northward and travels several miles up the North-eastern Ohio landscape to empty into the waters of the Great Lake itself, at the point where it bisects the city of Cleveland, Ohio. But just before it finds the more tranquil waters of the lake, the Cuyahoga splits off a mile or two upstream into a minor, eastward-flowing watershed. Today, the neighbourhoods surrounding this small detour tend to be more affluent, such as the rather pristine planned community of Shaker Heights. However, even today, these suburbs still bear scars of the area's much more sordid past, the years of economic blight, poverty, and crime that became ubiquitous in this area of Cleveland, alongside the name that the area took from the small watershed itself—Kingsbury Run. While economic fortunes have risen and (more often) fallen in the area, perhaps no period in the history of Kingsbury Run was more ignominious than the 1930s, during the height of the Great Depression.

But these scars are not all mere socio-economic metaphors. In some cases, they played out in genuine acts of grotesque physical violence against the poor and vulnerable citizens who found themselves unfortunate enough to have fallen into the poverty and urban blight of Kingsbury Run. And, though the area has seen violence in its past—and still does all too far often today—no example of these physical scars have held such a dark and entrenched place in the city's collective consciousness as the brutal acts of murder and mutilation carried out in the 1930s by the still-unknown serial killer who must be identified only by his tabloid-induced pseudonym—the Cleveland Torso Murderer. Or, perhaps some might prefer his alternate title, identifying him with not only the neighbourhood where he carried out his reign of terror but also more clearly capturing the madness and sadism with which he carved fear through the city: the Mad Butcher of Kingsbury Run.

The killer's exact number of victims is unclear. The official canonical accounts of the murders hold the total victim count at twelve. However, investigators have noted several more murders of similar method and M.O. in the area and around the same time, which has led some to suggest that the Torso Murderer's actual victim count could number as high as 20, or even greater. Even more tragically, only two of the at least twelve victims have been positively identified, with a third potentially identified, and the rest remaining John and Jane Does, buried without a name or familial send-off in non-descript potter's fields around Cleveland.

Somewhat strangely for serial murders, the Torso Killer did not appear to have a preference for sex, age, or race in his victims. His twelve "official" victims number 7 men and 5 women, and men and women both being represented among the list of his "possible" victims as well. His victims, though all adults, also seemed to span a wide range of ages and physical characteristics (though these physical characteristics were difficult to determine in some of these cases, for reasons that will become clear momentarily). The only consistent thread that comes through with regards to the murderer's choice of victim is not their sex, age, or physical description, but rather *who* they were within the broader social context of 1930s Cleveland. All of the Cleveland Torso Murderer's victims—both confirmed and unconfirmed—were "lower-class" targets, many of whom were or appeared to have been vagrants, the homeless, or sex workers, and all of whom were taken from the economically devastated area around Kingsbury Run.

The Great Depression of the 1930s left scores of run-down, impoverished, and dangerous urban areas across the United States and the world, and few areas were more obviously affected by the global economic crisis than the Kingsbury Run area of Cleveland. In the '30s, the area became infamous for its numerous shantytowns—often derided as "Hobo Jungles"—where hundreds of newly homeless workers, transients, prostitutes, criminals, victims of mental illness, and any other number of societal outcasts were forced to find shelter in vast homeless camps. The area was also adjacent to a notorious cluster of blocks known as the "Roaring Third," a downtrodden area that at the time was infamous for its saturation of saloons, brothels, gambling dens, and other malign establishments. As should come as no surprise, crime was rampant here, and violent murders among the area's disaffected residents were not remotely uncommon. Given the ubiquity of these murders, and the low salience of the poor who lived here, these murders were not exactly headline news, nor did they tend to reach the daily gossip of the city's more affluent communities. That, however, abruptly changed in 1935, when Kingsbury Run saw a string of murders so gruesome, bizarre, and sensational that, for a time, the "forgotten" vagrants of the area became the object of intense focus by the media, city government, and population as a whole. If for no other reason than macabre rubbernecking.

The first two "canonical" victims of the killer who would come to be known as the Cleveland Torso Murderer were found on the same day, on September 23, 1935. On that day, the bodies of two men were found in an area of Kingsbury Run known as Jackass Hill. The bodies lay around 30 feet apart, and both had been dismembered and mutilated to varying degrees. Both bodies, for example, were missing their heads (what will become a common theme) and, among other indignities, had both been emasculated (in more graphic terms, their penises and testicles had been removed). In addition, the bodies were both naked, drained of much of their blood, and bore marks of rope burns, suggesting that they had been bound before their deaths. More curiously, one of the bodies appeared to have been treated with some kind of chemical agent, possibly a disinfectant or embalming fluid, though this has never been determined definitively.

The heads of both men were later found dumped in different locations. Based upon facial features and fingerprint evidence, one of the bodies was identified as being that of Edward Andrassy, a young man who ostensibly had worked as a hospital orderly but who also had a somewhat notorious record around Kingsbury Run and the Roaring Third as a regular patron of the bars, brothels, and illegal casinos of the area. In providing their identification, the police noted that Andrassy "had been arrested many times for drunkenness, brawling, and carrying a concealed weapon. He was known to haunt the rougher areas around Kingsbury Run and had no steady job." The second victim, however, was never identified, and today is usually referred to only as "John Doe I" (in order to distinguish him from the body of numerous *John Does* that would soon begin to pile up as the killings of unidentified men continued).

The body of John Doe I was in a more advanced state of decomposition than that of Andrassy, and the coroner later estimated that, at the time of their discovery, Andrassy had been dead for only two to three days, while John Doe I had been dead for around three weeks. Thus, police concluded that John Doe I had been the murderer's first victim and Andrassy the second. Both victims, however, appear to have been dumped at Jackass Hill at the same time, suggesting that the killer had access to a secure location in which to store their bodies for a time.

Another few months would pass before more of the murderer's "work" was discovered. On January 26, 1936, the body of the middle-aged woman was found along Cleveland's Orange Avenue, a short distance from Kingsbury Run. Like the first two bodies, this one was also naked and dismembered, with the head, in particular, missing from the remains that were found. The woman's head, as with the first two victims, was found later on in a different location. This allowed police to positively identify the victim as Florence Polillo, a waitress, barmaid, and sometimes sex worker who lived and worked around some of the seedier establishments of the Roaring Third. The placement of Polillo's body was also somewhat notable, as her remains were found in plain sight next to the Hart Manufacturing Building, wrapped in old newspapers and placed in wooden baskets. At the very least, this suggested that the killer was becoming bolder in terms of where he left the bodies of his victims, perhaps *wanting* them to be found as he searched for some kind of perverse "fame." Tragically, Polillo would also be the last of the Torso Murderer's victims to be definitively identified. With the exception of one possible ID, all subsequent victims associated with the case would only be posthumously marked with a string of *John* and *Jane* Does, each bearing a numerical marker that bore a more and more tragic connotation as the number grew in quantity over time.

 Over the next two years, nine more bodies would be found around the Kingsbury Run area of Cleveland. The exact means by which the killer disposed of the bodies changed somewhat, as did the apparent conspicuousness with which he wanted his victims to be found. Some remains had been placed in highly public areas around Kingsbury Run, leading to quick discovery. Others were dumped in the Cuyahoga River, the woods, or on the shores of Lake Erie, farther out of sight of the public. Additionally, some victims were located soon after their killing, allowing for clearer determination of their facial features. Others, though, were not found until months later, at which point their remains had decomposed to mere bones.

 However, all cases bore nearly identical signatures. All had been dismembered in varying degrees, with the killer taking particular care to decapitate all of his victims. The dismembered remains were always separated so that only parts of a victim's body were discovered. In some cases, the head of a victim was never found, leading the coroner to only determine the sex and age range based on parts of a heavily decomposed torso or limb. The coroner did note that the dismemberment of the bodies appeared to have been done by an "expert" in surgery and anatomy rather than a mere amateur crudely dismembering victims without any precision or skill. This detail led to one of the first major details in the murderer's profile—the killer would likely have some kind of medical, surgical, or similar type of anatomical training.

Given that Edward Andrassy and Florence Polillo—the two identified victims—were impoverished and/or vagrant residents of the blighted Kingsbury Run area, and given that none of the victims could be identified based upon missing person reports or clear records, police assumed that all victims had likewise been drawn from the same pool of the homeless, transients, sex workers, and other vulnerable people found among the large poverty-stricken community in Kingsbury Run. If the murderer deliberately preyed upon the homeless or the transient, he would likely be assured that few would ever even be reported missing, having no loved ones or concerned friends who would recognize their absence. This lack of clear victim ID also frustrated the police investigation as a whole.

One *possible* identification came from the eighth victim, a woman whose skeletal remains were found beneath Cleveland's Lorain-Carnegie Bridge on June 6, 1937. Going off of incomplete dental records, police believed that this victim was likely a woman named Rose Wallace, who had been reported missing by her son ten months earlier. However, this ID remains inconclusive, as the dentist from whom the dental records were taken was dead when the body was found, and the records he had kept were not an insufficient condition to provide an exact match to the teeth found in the victim's skull in the state in which it was found. The timeline there also does not quite match up, as the coroner estimated that the woman's death had occurred over a year earlier, while Rose Wallace had only been missing for ten months. This, of course, could be reconciled by a number of factors that could have affected the coroner's estimated time of death and the body's decomposition process. Today, several experts on the case, as well as Wallace's own family, believe that this victim was indeed Rose Wallace.

If these crimes could be said to have any kind of "silver lining," it might be that the horrifying and grotesque nature of the murders and subsequent dismemberments finally got the broader culture of the city of Cleveland to take note of its destitute underclass, though here more as a sideshow attraction than as subjects who warranted humane and dignified consideration. As each new body was found, the Cleveland press, so used to simply ignoring the city's underclasses, suddenly descended into a frenzy of sensationalistic yellow journalism, detailing all of the grisly facts that they could find (and in some cases simply manufacturing them out of thin air), all the while excoriating the Cleveland police for their failure to make any leads in the case.

On the surface, the Cleveland Police may have appeared more suited than those of most other American cities to tackle such a daring yet mysterious fiend as the Torso Murderer proved to be. After all, Cleveland had a particular ace in its hole when it came to crime-fighting. During the 1930s, legendary law enforcement officer Eliot Ness—who had already achieved national fame as a Prohibition-era agent and as the seemingly fearless and incorruptible leader of the "Untouchables"—served as Cleveland's Director of Public Safety, giving him authority over the Cleveland police and all related services. Having taken on scores of violent criminals, including notorious Chicago mobster Al Capone, and *won*, Ness would seem to be well-equipped to take down a ghastly killer such as the one now terrorizing Kingsbury Run. And yet, as each new victim found their way into the papers, and police seemed no closer to even identifying potential suspects, let alone bringing them to justice, public opinion began to turn somewhat. Could it be, citizens whispered, that Ness was *not* the undefeatable force for law and justice that his image held him to be? This chatter must surely have gotten to Ness himself and filtered down through the entire Cleveland police department, who got more and more desperate to find any kind of lead in the case.

And, it would seem, the killer *himself* knew this. The remains of the final two canonical victims, an unidentified man, and woman, were both found on August 16, 1938, placed conspicuously on Cleveland's East 9th Street in direct view of Ness's office in city hall.

In what some have interpreted as an act of determined desperation, Ness himself led a small army of Cleveland police on a raid of one of the largest shantytowns of Kingsbury Run a mere two days after the discovery of the two latest victims in such close proximity to his office. Ness and his men tore through the so-called "Hobo Jungle" in a rather haphazard search for clues. Finding none, Ness then made an extremely controversial call and, citing dubious legal authority, ordered his officers to set fire to the entire encampment. By the end of the day, most of the makeshift shacks in the camps had been burned to the ground. Then, having destroyed the only "home" that the camp's residents knew, Ness ordered his officers to arrest the mass of the now-homeless citizens for the crime of "vagrancy." In his own account, Ness attempted to defend this action as an act of pre-emptive altruism. According to his somewhat tortured logic, Ness thought that destroying the pool of potential victims would prevent the killer from finding new targets and ultimately protect the destitute residents of Kingsbury Run from becoming dismembered corpses in the future. Ness also asserted that the mass arrest was actually a ploy to get the fingerprints of many of these vagrants on a police file in case they would be needed to identify new victims in the future. Still, most later commentators on this case have condemned the cruel and draconian nature of this tactic, and today this episode remains perhaps the most controversial aspect of Ness's otherwise lauded career.

And then, after the murderer's final taunt against Ness, the killings just…stopped. Or, at least, none of the anonymous bodies found in Cleveland's Kingsbury Run bore those specific species of pre-and post-mortem violence. Murders of unidentified vagrants from Kingsbury Run continued, of course, but none bore the precise, calculated mutilation and dismemberment that marked the reign of terror of the Torso Killer. That being said, later investigations have revealed several more killings that could potentially be connected to the case, sharing similarities in M.O., location, and timeline. The most notable of these is a female victim commonly referred to as the "Lady of the Lake." This victim was found on September 5, 1934, more than a year before the discovery of the first two canonical victims. The woman's remains were located on the shores of Lake Erie, near a Cleveland-area amusement park called Euclid Lake. As with the Torso Murderer's canonical victims, the Lady of the Lake's body was dismembered and decapitated, with only her torso, thighs, and a few other dismembered body parts being recovered. Like so many of the canonical victims, her head was never found. Even more curiously, later research into this case found that her remains may have been treated with a chemical agent similar to that found on the body of John Doe I when it was found at Jackass Hill a year later. These details have led many case experts to include this woman as one of the Torso Murderer's "official" victims, though this remains somewhat controversial.

Additional victims were also found in areas around the city of Pittsburgh in Western Pennsylvania in the years before and after the Cleveland Torso Murders. In 1936, a man's headless body was found in a boxcar near the city of New Castle, Pennsylvania, a bit north of Pittsburgh. Human remains had also been found in some of the swamps around New Castle going back to at least 1921, though none were ever identified. In 1940, three more headless bodies were found in a boxcar in the borough of McKees Rocks, just outside Pittsburgh. All of these areas were within a relatively short train ride from Cleveland for any of the various transients of the time who were known to ride the rails. Finally, on July 22, 1950, twelve years after the last of the Torso Murderer's canonical killings, a decapitated body later determined to be that of 44-year-old Robert Robertson was found on Cleveland's Davenport Avenue. Given the similarities in method and location, many in the press were quick to jump on stories of the "Mad Butcher's return." However, no definitive link between this murder and the earlier torso killings was ever established by police.

Despite the intense media coverage and years-long police investigation, only two suspects were ever seriously considered in the case. However, these two suspects do bring to the forefront a rather grave whisper of conspiracy, coverup, and dark intrigue in ways that have haunted and disturbed those who have looked back on this case from the present day. The potential conspiracies associated with this case have become almost as infamous as the gruesome nature of the killings themselves and add another layer to the Cleveland Torso Murderer's status as one of the most lasting and fascinating of all unsolved crimes.

The first suspect to receive serious attention from police was a man named Frank Dolezal. Dolezal came to the attention of investigators as a potential suspect in 1939, following years of intense frustration, mockery, and pent-up rage as the case still went unsolved with each passing day. Dolezal was, at the time, a 52-year-old resident of Kingsbury Run, with a reputation for being something of a "strange" and off-putting figure. According to residents of the area, Dolezal was known to collect knives and say bizarre and potentially threatening things to people whom he knew. But police did not consider him their prime suspect until they discovered that he was a close friend and former roommate of Florence Polillo, the killer's third known victim. What's more, evidence also came out that he may have known Edward Andrassy as well, in addition to other missing Kingsbury Run residents who had been considered possible identities of some of the other victims.

With pressure mounting on them, police arrested Dolezal on August 24, 1939, ostensibly for the murder of Florence Polillo. Once in custody, Dolezal actually signed a confession claiming responsibility for Polillo's murder, as well as the other murders in the case. However, he later recanted this, claiming that his "confession" had, in fact, been the result of excessive violence and abuse by the police themselves. Indeed, a later medical examination revealed several large bruises across his body and broken ribs, suggesting that he had indeed been the victim of a violent assault while in police custody. Later investigations also reveal that much of the information about the case that Dolezal "provided" was quite inaccurate, and that the police had "coached" him on some of the main details of the killings. Unfortunately, Dolezal would never see justice for this—while he was awaiting trial for Polillo's killing, Dolezal was found dead in his Cuyahoga County Jail cell. Officially, his cause of death was suicide by hanging. However, given the rather strong evidence that he had been railroaded into signing a false confession by means of police violence, many people today dispute suicide as his actual cause of death.

The possibility of a police conspiracy and coverup to frame Dolezal for the murders overshadowed, for a time, the *other* major suspect in the case. And this one, unlike Dolezal, drew interest from the highest authorities in the investigation. In recent years, contemporary investigators of the Cleveland Torso Murders, most notable journalist James Jessen Badal, uncovered evidence that Eliot Ness himself had found a "secret suspect," whom he personally believed to be the murderer. According to unsealed records, Ness, taking personal charge of the case as the body count grew, had apparently personally detained a man by the name of Dr. Francis E. Sweeney for a lengthy, albeit secret, interrogation. In fact, Ness had Sweeney sequestered in a hotel room for several days, many of which were apparently needed just to get a drunken Sweeney sober enough for a coherent interrogation. During this time, Sweeney seems to have *failed early* versions of a polygraph test when attempting to deny that he knew anything about the killings. The polygraph administrator (the actual co-inventor of the polygraph Leonarde Keeler) was quite certain based upon these results that Ness had gotten his man.

Ness, however, disagreed. Part of this was the flimsy nature of the polygraph as a form of evidence at the time (indeed, even today, it is not exactly admissible in court, and only ever used as a means of gaining further evidence or a confession), and partly because Ness's entire secret detention and interrogation of Sweeney would likely be thrown out of court on the basis of being a clear violation of Sweeney's civil liberties. Another potentially thorny issue was the fact that Dr. Sweeney was, in fact, the first cousin of Congressman Martin L. Sweeney, a powerful politician representing the Cleveland area and one who had publicly accosted Ness and the Cleveland Police for their failure to capture the Torso Murderer. Ness, unable to build a case that he believed would hold up in court, and fearing potential political reprisals from Sweeney's powerful family, was forced to let him go, but apparently never lost his strong suspicion that he had, in that hotel room, the Cleveland Torso Murderer himself.

So, just who was Dr. Francis E. Sweeney that made him such a strong suspect in the eyes of Ness and many of the contemporary investigators of these crimes? Given the lack of clear records (as Ness's investigation and detention of Sweeney was, of course, both secretive and likely illegal), no one knows how Ness himself came to view Sweeney as a prime suspect. However, a cursory glance at Sweeney himself reveals several disturbing details. On the surface, Dr. Sweeney was a fairly upstanding member of Cleveland's community. A practicing physician and veteran of the First World War, Sweeney enjoyed a seemingly happy home life with a wife and several children. However, not far beneath the surface, darkness lurked. Sweeney, despite his gilded exterior, bore deeper psychological dysfunction, which manifested themselves in severe alcoholism and violent outbursts. In fact, Sweeney's wife later revealed that he was known to be violent and physically abusive with her and their children and often showed concerning signs of mental instability and even psychosis.

In terms of the basic profile of the Torso Murderer, Dr. Sweeney would seem to be a solid match. As a doctor, Sweeney would have the necessary medical and surgical skills to perform the "expert" mutilations and dismemberments of his victims. What's more, during his military service in the First World War, Sweeney had been part of a medical unit that specifically performed amputations on wounded soldiers. Thus, even before entering into his medical practice in Cleveland, Sweeney would have more than enough experience in anatomy and amputation to perform the kinds of expert dismemberments found on the Torso Murderer victims.

In addition to the fact that Sweeney was a doctor with clear violent and psychopathic tendencies, contemporary investigators have also uncovered a great deal of circumstantial evidence that would closely tie Sweeney to the torso killings. Based upon statements provided by Sweeney's wife, Sweeney would apparently go missing from both his family and his practice for extended periods, often days at a time. Contemporary Cleveland journalist and researcher James Jessen Badal has since looked at these statements and compared them to the timeline of the torso murders as they were constructed by police and coroner evidence. The result, he found, was a strong correspondence between Sweeney's temporary disappearances and when the abductions and killings would have been performed. Additionally, Sweeney's medical practice was located near the Kingsbury Run area of Cleveland, and many of his patients would likely have been drawn from the very same pool of impoverished transients that served as the main victim pool for the Torso Killer. Badal also found that Sweeney's medical office was located next to a funeral parlour. If Sweeney had made a surreptitious agreement with the parlour's funeral director to use his facilities for surgical practice on cadavers—a somewhat common practice among doctors and funeral parlours at the time—then Sweeney could have used these facilities and their instruments as a secret means of dismembering the bodies of his victims and disposing of the excessive amounts of blood and other bodily mess without raising any suspicions.

In addition, Badal uncovered a previously-forgotten police report from the time during which the murders were occurring. In 1938, a Kingsbury Run vagrant apparently by the name of *Emil* seems to have gone to the police and told them a somewhat incoherent story about a "doctor" who had tried to drug him in 1934. Why exactly this man waited four years to go to the police with his story is unclear, but the officers undoubtedly used to dealing with the homeless and transient population of the area and thus less than sympathetic, briefly humoured the man by offering him a ride to the area where he was supposedly almost drugged and abducted. "Emil" couldn't quite remember the exact location but did take the police to a circle of city blocks around Broadway Street and between 50th and 55th Streets in Cleveland. However, once there, the officers were unable to find anything resembling a doctor's office, and, losing patience with the homeless man, eventually kicked him out of their car and dismissed his story as nothing more than the rantings of a crazy hobo.

However, in 2001, James Badal, while researching for his book about the Torso Murders, discovered a shocking piece of evidence—Francis Sweeney actually *did have* a medical office in 1934 in the exact area that Emil had taken police in his vain search for the spot where he was almost drugged and abducted.

And it seems that Sweeney never quite forgot his "detention" and secret interrogation by Eliot Ness. For years afterward, Sweeney sent Ness several rambling and mocking postcards, seeming to rub Ness's face into his failure to apprehend the Torso Murderer. If Sweeney was, in fact, the killer, this would line up well with the final insult that the killer sent to Ness—leaving his final two victims in direct sight of Ness's office.

But perhaps the most haunting piece of evidence implicating Sweeney in the crimes is how the killing spree ended. In late 1938, Sweeney, having already been diagnosed with a traumatic stress disorder leftover from his service in the First World War, checked himself into a mental hospital. Here, he was diagnosed with schizophrenia and kept on a psychiatric hold for several years. It was during this confinement that Sweeney sent most of his mocking letters to Ness, hinting that he might be the killer, but never providing any sufficient statement that could actually incriminate him. But, more importantly, is how this lines up with the timeline of the killings. The last two canonical victims—the two that were found in sight of Ness's city hall office—were discovered on August 16, 1938. A few weeks later, Sweeney checked himself into a mental hospital and began a multi-year stay. After this, the killings stopped.

Ultimately, with no fresh bodies to drive media sensationalism, the case gradually fell out of the public consciousness. Occasional gruesome crimes in the general area around Cleveland would bring up comparisons to the Torso Killer, or speculation that the killer had "returned," but these never amounted to much. Ness died in 1957 at his retirement home in Coudersport, Pennsylvania. Francis Sweeney died in a veteran's hospital in 1964. In 2010, James Jessen Badal and other benefactors purchased a marker for Frank Dolezal's grave, marked with a simple inscription: *Rest Now.*

Chapter 13
The Infamous Hinterkaifeck Murders

Despite its current tranquil status as a peaceful and prosperous European power, the nation of Germany is no stranger to a number of horrific and tragic events over the past hundred years, as anyone vaguely familiar with history will know. Still, the largescale horrors brought on by both World Wars, the Holocaust, and the Cold War can sometimes overshadow smaller horrors, miniature in death count but certainly not in their ability to induce dread or cold chills among any subsequent investigator who happens to come across their details in the annals of history.

One such case is the infamous murders of Hinterkaifeck farm. Though almost a century old at this point, the gruesome mass killing of a farmstead's entire family and household staff remains one of the most infamous unsolved crimes in the history of Germany. And this status is not only due to the violent and sadistic nature of the murders themselves or the fact that the case remains unsolved to this day. Rather, the case also stands out among the vast annals of unsolved crimes for a number of concomitant details that are somewhat...strange, to say the least. Strange, downright disturbing, and potentially even *paranormal*, depending upon how one looks at them.

The setting for the crime could also not have been creepier. Built in 1863, the Hinterkaifeck farm lay in the sparsely-populated fields and leftover forests of rural Bavaria, about 70 kilometres north of Munich. The farm in question lay a little more than two kilometres behind, or "hinter," the small hamlet of Kaifeck. This provided the farmland with the name by which the location and the crime itself would come to be known.

By the early 1920s, the farmstead was under the ownership of one Andreas Gruber. Gruber was an older and somewhat reclusive figure in the local community, one who may be fated, in a sense, to spawn gossip and rumours, regardless of his actual character (indeed, the whispers about him that had floated throughout the town long before the murders would become pertinent to the case itself). Gruber, aged 63 at the time of his death, shared the house with his wife Cäzilia (age 72), their daughter Viktoria (age 35), and Viktoria's two young children (seven-year-old Cäzilia, nicknamed "Cäzey," and two-year-old Joseph). The house also held quarters for a single maid, who would live and work on the property.

Viktoria Gruber's husband, and Andreas Gruber's son-in-law, Karl Gabriel, had ostensibly been killed in France during the First World War, leaving Viktoria widowed with a young daughter. However, Gabriel's body had never officially been recovered, leading to subsequent rumours that he had not actually died at all. This path of speculation would, again, become relevant during the subsequent murder investigation. Also of note regarding Viktoria's late husband was the fact that she had borne young Joseph well *after* her late husband's supposed death. As with the issue of Karl Gabriel's death, the unanswered question of who fathered young Joseph would soon become darkly relevant.

For the farmlands of Bavaria, the winter of 1922 lingered well beyond its time, and many a farmer woke up on March mornings to the unpleasant sight of a fresh layer of snow cast across his fields. The cold and dreary atmosphere of what was supposed to be springtime would come to serve as the perfect setting for what would eventually be found at the Hinterkaifeck farm come early April.

The townsfolk around Kaifeck first began to notice that something may be off with the Gruber family shortly after March 31. For a few days, young Cäzey had not shown up to school, and no word from her parents had come in with an official excuse. What's more, the family, known to be regular church-goers, had not shown up for Sunday service. In their isolation at the edge of town, the Gruber family had already borne a number of murky rumours among the residents of the surrounding area, so their sudden disappearance from their normal public life may have elicited a degree of concern among the people who would come closest to being counted as their "neighbours." Still, reports came in over the next few days that seemed to put things at ease, at least initially. A few people passing by the Hinterkaifeck farmstead reported seeing smoke rising from the chimney of the house, indicating that someone was there to start a fire and maintain it.

But other reports began to come in that perhaps warranted a bit more concern. On April 1, two traveling coffee salesmen had reportedly gone to the house to take the Gruber family's order. However, despite knocking on the door and the windows for an extended period, no one came to answer, and the pair eventually left with their orders unfulfilled. The two did apparently note that the gate leading to the farm's engine room had been left open, though they did not investigate this further.

On April 4, a repairman arrived at the farm to do some prearranged repairs to the farm's food chopper. However, he, too, did not encounter any members of the family, nor did anyone from the house come out to greet him or respond when he knocked. After an hour's wait, the repairman eventually decided to go about his repairs without checking in with them, remaining there for an additional four hours and still encountering no one else on the property. During this time, he did note that the animals in the barn were still present, and appeared to have been fed recently.

Later that day, the Gruber's nearest neighbour, a widower named Lorenz Schlittenbauer, had grown sufficiently concerned with the lack of any contact with the family that he sent his son and stepson to the Hinterkaifeck property in an attempt to get confirmation of their wellbeing. Like the other visitors of the past few days, however, the boys were unable to make contact with anyone on the property.

Growing ever more concerned, Schlittenbauer decided to go to the farm himself, bringing two other Kaifeck residents named Jakob Sigl and Michael Pöll. When the three were once again unable to get anyone to answer the door or respond to knocks and shouts through the windows, they decided to make a more thorough search of the property. This search would eventually lead them into the main barn attached to the house. What they would find there continues to haunt the small, quaint area to the present day.

    Inside the barn were the bodies of Andreas, Cäzilia, Viktoria, and Cäzey. The three adults were found all piled on top of each other and crammed onto a cluster of hay, while young Cäzey was found propped up against a wall in the corner. All four bodies showed signs of extreme violence. Andreas, for example, was only identifiable thanks to his large, dark moustache—pretty much everything else on this face had been viciously beaten into a bloody, unrecognizable pulp. Cäzilia and Viktoria had also had their heads and faces bludgeoned without mercy, with Viktoria also showing dark bruising around her neck that suggested her killer may have attempted to strangle her as well. Viktoria's fatal wounds were found in her torso, though the first wave of responders noted that the young girl's body still clutched chunks of hair in its hands. Disturbingly, later medical examination of the body showed that the little girl had likely survived her initial injuries and remained trapped in the barn with the remains of her mother and grandparents as she slowly bled out. The psychological trauma of this may have induced her to pull out her own hair, though some have speculated that the hair may have belonged to her attacker, whom she attempted to fight off.

    Following this gruesome discovery, Schlittenbauer, Sigl, and Pöll broke into the house itself to try and find any evidence of potential survivors of whatever horrific act of violence had transpired there. Unfortunately, they only found more bodies. In the house's maid chamber, they found the body of 44-year-old Maria Baumgartner, who, in a terrible stroke of luck, had only begun her job as the family's maid that very day. Her body was found in its bed, still dressed in her nightclothes, suggesting that her killer had attacked her when she was still in bed. After bashing her skull in, the killer proceeded to shove her body haphazardly underneath her mattress. Elsewhere in the house, the trio found the body of two-year-old Joseph, who had been likewise bludgeoned to death in his crib.

Following this discovery, the three men were, of course, immediately compelled to contact the authorities. Unfortunately, due to the limits of 1920s communication technology and the farmhouse's remote location, the Munich police did not get to the farmhouse until several hours after the discovery of the bodies. By this point, much of the population of the surrounding town had beaten them there, and the entire crime scene had become something of a macabre tourist attraction. Frustratingly, many of these would-be rubberneckers had taken it upon themselves to move the bodies around, rearrange potential pieces of evidence in the farmhouse, and even help themselves to food inside the house itself. Thus, the actual criminal investigation was somewhat hampered from the start, even by the relatively lax standards of the 1920s.

Still, the police did what they could. The initial autopsy, performed on the bodies while they still lay in the barn, concluded that the murder weapon had likely been a mattock, a farming instrument similar to a pickaxe. No such instrument was found at the scene, however, so for the time being, that line of inquiry appeared to be a dead-end. Meanwhile, police began interviewing any potential witnesses or suspects, attempting to gain as clear a picture as possible of the events leading up to the murder itself or who may have had the motive to commit such a horrific act.

During this initial investigation, authorities uncovered a few of the more disturbing details that have elevated this case in the minds of true-crime aficionados up to the present day. Based upon reports from those who had been in contact with the Grubers during the weeks leading up to their murder, the family had apparently been experiencing several strange occurrences at the farm. For months, many members of the household had reported hearing strange noises throughout the house, including muffled voices and footsteps coming from the attic. In fact, these occurrences eventually got so bad that the family's former maid resigned from her job out of fear that the house was haunted (her eventual replacement was the ill-fated Maria Baumgartner, who would be repaid for her service with a mattock to the head at the end of her first day).

Other neighbours heard reports of supposed vandalism. For example, Andreas Gruber had been overheard complaining that someone had attempted to break into his farm's engine room a few days before his murder, though he had never caught the supposed perpetrator. He also apparently had had one of his keys stolen and had found a newspaper in his house that neither he nor anyone in his family read or subscribed to.

But the most alarming detail came a short while before the final, violent act. On one of the mornings where the lingering March winter had dumped a fresh layer of snow across the area the previous night, Andrea awoke to discover a set of footprints leading from the nearby woods right up to his house. Footprints that *only* came up to his house, revealing no indication that this visitor, whoever they may be, had ever left. A search of the house had apparently turned up nothing, but suffice to say, the Gruber family had some reason to be on edge during the last few days of their lives.

Even more disturbingly, police quickly came to the conclusion that the murderer, rather than fleeing from the sight of his horrific act while the blood still settled on the ground, had, in fact, *stayed* at the house for several days afterward. In addition to the sight of smoke rising from the chimney of the house during the time at which the Gruber family would have been lying dead in their barn, police also found that the farm's animals had been fed, the property maintained somewhat, and food from the kitchen had even been eaten as late as the day before the discovery (though, part of this could be ascribed to the afore-mentioned town gawkers who helped themselves to the slain family's food while awaiting the police).

The attempt at a criminal investigation over the next week or so was plagued with several issues and blunders that hampered any hope of identifying a suspect. Fingerprint evidence, then still in its infancy as forensic science, was completely out of the question given how contaminated the crime scene had become before the police even got there. The bodies were eventually taken to Munich for further examination. However, in a somewhat impressive display of bureaucratic incompetence, the heads of all six victims (removed for further study) were *all* lost. When the six victims were eventually given funeral proceedings and burial a week later, none of their heads were buried with them. What's more, detectives focused a bit too much of their initial interrogations on random passers-by and petty criminals that had been known to the area, rather than attempting to deduce any potential suspect who would have been familiar enough to the Gruber family to lure them into such a sense of security.

This latter point would not prove to be an insignificant one. With little evidence of an actual struggle in the house itself, later investigators concluded that the four victims found in the barn had gone there willingly, suggesting that they had somehow been lured by someone whom they knew. Instead of going this route, police initially proclaimed the motive of the crime to have been a robbery, likely committed by a passing vagrant, despite the fact that a rather large amount of money and valuables were still safe and sound in the house.

Though the initial investigation was botched pretty thoroughly, two main suspects eventually emerged in the years and decades following the ghastly crime. Both suspects, as it happened, related to the lingering question of who fathered young Joseph, the toddler son of Viktoria born years after her husband had supposedly died a wartime casualty of the Western Front. In fact, the first such theory posits that that very husband, the late Karl Gabriel, was not actually *late* after all. As Gabriel's body was never actually recovered from the artillery attack that supposedly killed him, some have theorized that he had somehow managed to fake his death and flee the German army for the rest of the war. In this account, Gabriel eventually made his way back to Hinterkaifeck in 1922, only to find his wife Viktoria having borne a child with another man. In his subsequent rage, he massacred not only his wife and her bastard son but his actual daughter, his parents-in-law, and the family maid as well, just for good measure.

A second theory seems somewhat more plausible, though it too lacks any direct evidence. Ever since Joseph's illegitimate birth, the townsfolk around Kaifeck had whispered that the family's closest neighbour, the widower Lorenz Schlittenbauer, had actually been young Joseph's father. There *does* seem to be evidence that Schlittenbauer had a noticeable degree of affection for Viktoria, though it seems as if Andreas himself forbade any kind of marriage between the two. As Schlittenbauer also happened to be the first one to discover their bodies, it didn't take long for investigators to look at him as the prime suspect. Of course, Schlittenbauer had his own farm to maintain and thus would not likely have had the time to not only make his way over to the Gruber's farm and murder the entire family but then remain in the house for several days afterward.

Finally, many theories and leads pertaining to the case ultimately come back to one of the darkest and most prevalent rumours about the Gruber family itself, one that had circled around the town long before they met their untimely end. For years, suspicions had been raised among the townsfolk that the relationship between old Andreas Gruber and Viktoria was *more* than a normal relationship between father and daughter. As if the general charge of incest were not enough, some had even come to believe that

Andreas *himself* was the biological father of young Joseph, taking the role of both father *and* grandfather. These rumours were never substantiated, nor has any direct connection between (alleged) incest in the Gruber family and their ultimate murder ever been established. Still, gruesome rumours and gruesome crimes tend to find each other sooner or later, and one imagines that few of the townsfolk around Kaifeck were particularly surprised when they found out which family had fallen victim to a crime of such a shocking nature.

Chapter 14
21st Century UFO Sightings

The modern conception of UFO sightings can generally be placed around the early-to-mid 20th Century. Not that there weren't sightings of unknown objects in the sky before this. In fact, accounts exist going back to the earliest days of recorded history that describe strange things seen in an otherwise empty sky. Pre-modern peoples, however, tended to interpret these sightings as "angels," "gods," or in other religious or mythological terms. It was not until the 20th Century and its advent of the possibility of human space flight that a UFO sighting brought forth the possibility of an alien race visiting Earth from another planet.

But while many of the best-known UFO sightings—Roswell, Kenneth Arnold, the supposed abduction of Betty and Barney Hill, etc.—are relics of the 20th Century, the opening two decades of the 21st Century have seen their share of credible and mystifying UFO encounters as well.

One of the first major UFO sightings, at least in the United States, occurred in the summer of 2001. In most circumstances, few sections of the New Jersey Turnpike are worth pulling over for. The small section surrounding the New Jersey town of Carteret is certainly no exception to this rule. Located in Northern Jersey, Carteret is mainly surrounded by the same menagerie of smokestacks, townhouses, and strip malls as most of the rest of the area. At that point on the Turnpike, motorists would most often have little to gaze upon other than the expanse of Staten Island lying across the Arthur Kill channel, with the glitzy lights and skyscrapers of Manhattan barely visible in the distance.

But just after midnight in the early hours of July 14, 2001, the few drivers unfortunate enough to find themselves on that stretch of the turnpike at that ungodly hour were treated to something else entirely.

Though no known footage exists of the incident, multiple witnesses reported nearly identical accounts of the phenomenon at the same time. On a basic level, what witnesses reported seeing in the sky over the New Jersey Turnpike were "lights." Several of them, in fact. A local police officer who witnessed the event counted the lights at sixteen. According to most reports, the lights were coloured a kind of "red-orange" and seemed to float gracefully across the night sky. Eyewitnesses reported that some of these lights were arranged in a *V* shape, bringing up possible comparisons to the infamous 1997 "Phoenix Lights" UFO incident from a few years earlier. The most common report specifies that a group of the lights maintained a clear *V* shape in the middle of the cluster, while the remaining lights seemed to group around them in a clear—and seemingly deliberate—arrangement.

One thing that is also notable about this sighting is not merely the UFOs themselves but also the effect that they seem to have had upon those who witnessed them. Many drivers found themselves compelled to pull over to the side of the road to get a clearer view of the objects hovering in the sky above them. Some even reported being overcome with a sudden feeling of intense peace or serenity, likening it to a kind of religious experience. For this reason, some witnesses interpreted the lights, not as evidence of alien intelligence visiting Earth but rather a "miraculous" occurrence sent from the heavens.

Though the exact direction and location of the lights were hard to determine from the ground, most witnesses reported that the lights seemed to be moving slowly along the trajectory of the Arthur Kill waterway separating New Jersey from New York. And then, the lights just…vanished. After floating across the sky for several minutes, the lights—according to most witness accounts—began to "flicker," and eventually faded away one by one, until there was once more nothing left in the night sky save for the wayward clouds and whatever stars can be seen against the ubiquitous light pollution from New York City.

Regardless, at least 15 calls to 911 were catalogued reporting the strange lights. Curiously, air traffic control at the nearby Newark International Airport has "officially" reported that their radar indicated no unusual activity within their airspace outside the normal air traffic for that hour of the night. However, a group called New York Strange Phenomena Investigators later claimed that they were able to uncover suppressed evidence from FAA radar at Newark, indicating that, on the night of the sighting, there had in fact been "an enormous number of airborne objects, without transponders, beginning at 10:31 PM and ending at 12:51 AM EST." How this group came upon this information, or how credible it is, is unclear.

One possible explanation for this particular phenomenon is that the lights were merely military flares released during an Air Force training exercise. This, after all, was a purported explanation for the similar Phoenix Lights sighting from a few years earlier. This *would* explain a few details from the case, such as the specific coloration of the lights and how they seemed to flicker and fade away after a few minutes. However, as with the Phoenix Lights, there are also some flaws in this explanation. For one, the military flares theory does not explain the apparent pattern and grouping of the lights, according to most eyewitness testimony. Recall that most witnesses—including more credible reports from police officers—held that many of the lights were clearly organized in a *V* shape, with the remaining one clustered around them in what looked like a deliberate and organized pattern. This clear formation would be highly unlikely with mere airborne flares, which would float randomly at the discretion of the wind and elements rather than staying in a coherent and organized pattern. Another problem is the fact that no evidence of any such military exercise from the area has ever been found. Though often kept somewhat secret, standard training exercises are not usually the kind of thing that the military keeps classified. Thus, if these flares *were* the result of U.S. military activity, what exactly was the military up to that night that would require this degree of secrecy? Certainly something far more significant than an air force flare exercise.

The 2001 New Jersey Turnpike sighting is also notable for a particular turn from most of the more infamous UFO incidents from the 20th Century. Rather than relegated to sparsely-populated areas in the desert or underdeveloped woodlands, this particular sighting occurred over an extremely busy interstate highway within one of the world's largest metropolitan areas. This twist in UFO sightings would also come up again in 2006 when a UFO was once more spotted in a less-than-inconspicuous area, this time over one of the world's busiest airports.

On the afternoon of November 7, 2006, the ground crew at Chicago's O'Hare International Airport were as busy as ever, overseeing hundreds of flights arriving and departing with the necessary machine-like precision required for any busy airport. However, around 4:15 PM, a ground crew member saw something that almost brought the frenzied airspace to a standstill. While pushing a United Airlines flight from its gate in preparation for take-off, the ground crewmember suddenly saw what he described as a "metallic," "flying saucer-like object" that appeared to be hovering in the air directly above the airplane. The crew member reported it to the flight crew on the plane, who apparently also witnessed the strange object hovering above them. All in all, around twelve witnesses—mostly O'Hare ground crew and United Airlines flight crew aboard the plane—are recorded as having witnessed the object. Their reports were all nearly identical in the description. The object was "dark grey in colour" and was estimated to be somewhere between six feet (1.8 meters) to 24 feet (7.3 meters) in diameter. Based on these descriptions, the object's flat shape and metallic-like consistency would appear to correspond quite closely to the classic "flying saucer" UFO shape. However, despite the sighting being so shocking to witnesses that the ground crew almost immediately called the incident in to air traffic control over the radio, no pictures were apparently taken of the actual object.

Based upon most witness reports, however, the object continued to hover silently above the airplane for about five minutes before it abruptly shot upward vertically at an incredible speed, disappearing from sight in a matter of seconds. Witnesses later reported that the speed at which the object ascended was so great, it actually punched a visible hole in the cloud layer over the airport, allowing the ground crew and pilots to see the blue sky beyond it for a few minutes.

However, despite the urgency that this sighting bore in eyewitnesses, air traffic control and the American Federal Aviation Administration were less than convinced. O'Hare's air traffic control has repeatedly stated that they never saw evidence of any such craft appear on their radar, nor did they ever see any visual evidence during the time when it was supposedly sighted. (The point about the lack of radar evidence is apparently true, as the actual transcripts of air traffic control's communication with the FAA regarding the incident have been released via a Freedom of Information Act request). Eventually, the FAA declined to investigate the case further, citing the lack of any radar evidence, and speculated that it was most likely a somewhat unusual meteorological phenomenon that was misidentified. Indeed, a few weather experts and astronomers have pointed to a particular atmospheric phenomenon called a "hole-punch cloud," in which an otherwise solid cloud cover will be "punctured" with a circular hole that could, in the right circumstances, look like a flying saucer. For example, astronomer Mark Hammergren believed that the specific atmospheric conditions at O'Hare on the day of the sighting were the right conditions for hole-punch clouds to form, and that the occurrence is rare enough that even an experienced ground and flight crew would be unlikely to know what they were seeing.

That being said, the actual eyewitnesses have dismissed this explanation, remaining firm in their claim that what they saw was not a simple cloud formation or atmospheric phenomenon. Rather, the dozen or so witnesses have all been quite adamant that they did indeed see a clear, metallic-like object hovering for a few minutes over the gate and then suddenly rocketing at a nearly impossible speed up into the sky.

About a year and a half later, a similar sighting occurred, but this time the supposed UFO returned to its better-known hangout of the American Southwest. On the evening of January 8, 2008, residents of the small West Texas town of Stephenville suddenly reported a sighting of…something…in the sky above their town. The exact details of what they saw in the sky that evening vary somewhat from witness to witness. A few of the earlier-known witnesses said that what they saw was a single, massive craft or object of some sort, with some describing the object as vaguely saucer-shaped and about half a mile wide and a mile long—or "bigger than a Walmart," as one witness put it. These accounts would put the incident in a similar league as the sighting over O'Hare airport, in which a single, saucer-shaped craft hovered over an area for several minutes.

However, other witnesses to the Stephenville event described something more akin to the sighting over the New Jersey Turnpike in 2001. These witnesses claimed that, rather than a singular, large object, they saw several smaller objects, or "lights," that seemed to move through the sky in a kind of deliberate pattern or organization. The lights were commonly described as being a bright, almost fiery red—"the reddest things I've seen in the sky," a former U.S. Air Force officer was quoted as saying.

It should be noted here that many of the witnesses who initially reported a single, large object also reported several bright lights illuminating the side of the object, which could explain the discrepancy between witness reports somewhat. Assuming that the object's main mass was obscured by cloud or excess evening sunlight, some witnesses may only have been able to see the lights themselves at the angle from which they were watching, making the craft appear to be a string of organized but unconnected bright lights instead of a single large craft.

Regardless of discrepancies in witness reports as to the nature of the object (or objects) itself, a few details *were* consistent across many different accounts. For one, the UFO was consistently described as moving in ways that seemed to defy any known standard of aerospace engineering. Many witnesses reported that the object or objects were, at one minute, moving extremely slowly, or remaining stationary altogether, and then abruptly accelerating at a seemingly impossible rate, to a seemingly impossible speed. Steve Allen, an eyewitness who also happened to be an amateur pilot, noted that the object he saw cleared a distance in seconds that normally took him around 20 minutes to fly in his Cessna plane. Based on this, he estimated that the object had suddenly accelerated to a speed of around 3,000 miles per hour, which is beyond the capabilities of any known Earthly aircraft operating today (for comparison, the fastest-known aircraft, the Lockheed SR-71 Blackbird, has a top speed of around 2,100 miles per hour, about 900MPH slower than the speed at which this object supposedly moved).

Another consistent detail is that the aerial phenomenon, despite its high speeds, acceleration, and seemingly impossible manoeuvres, was apparently entirely *silent*. At the very least, the object/objects did not make any noise that was audible to anyone watching on the ground, something that most certainly would not be the case with the powerful (and loud) jet engines of any known aircraft that could come close to matching these movements or speeds.

Finally, many witnesses reported that the object, whatever it was, was eventually "pursued" by a group of military jet fighters that appeared to have been dispatched to intercept whatever was in the sky over West Texas that evening. According to these reports, however, the jet fighters were hopelessly outmatched, with the aerial phenomenon easily avoiding the U.S. military's most state-of-the-art aircrafts. In fact, one witness described the object as almost seeming to "toy" with the jet fights, appearing to deliberately get close to them and then suddenly shooting away when they began to approach.

And Stephenville *is* in relatively close proximity to several military airbases, most notably the Naval Air Station Joint Reserve Base Fort Worth. However, immediately after the sightings, the military command in the area first denied that any military aircrafts had been dispatched on the evening of January 8. This account was later revised, though. On January 23, almost two weeks after the sightings, the Air Force Reserve Command Public Affairs did release a statement reading: "Ten F-16s from the 457th Fighter Squadron were performing training operations from 6 to 8 pm on Jan. 8 in the Brownwood Military Operations Area, which includes the airspace above Erath County."

As previously mentioned, the military does tend to prefer a degree of discretion when discussing even anodyne training exercises. However, the initial denial, followed by a sudden reversal in the form of a carefully crafted statement, did not exactly lead to widespread faith in the veracity of the military's account of events that evening.

Though, the potential involvement of the military in this incident does raise a distinct possibility. What if the object or objects sighted by Stephenville residents on the evening of January 8 were not *extra-terrestrial* crafts, as some have argued, but rather experimental crafts being tested and operated by their own government? For much of the 20th Century's UFO frenzy, experimental military technologies have been a somewhat common alternative explanation for strange aerial phenomena. And, in this case, the possibility would make a bit more sense than either the New Jersey Turnpike or O'Hare sightings. After all, if the

United States military *were* testing experimental aircraft of a kind previously unseen, they would reasonably prefer to do so in the somewhat rural and sparsely-populated areas of West Texas—especially if those areas are in the convergence zone of multiple military bases—than in the much more heavily-populated areas around the New York metropolitan area or Chicago's O'Hare Airport.

Regardless, the U.S. military most emphatically did *not* make any comment confirming the existence of UFOs during this supposed training exercise or that the aircraft in question had been dispatched specifically to intercept something peculiar that had appeared on radar. This, however, was not the case for what would arguably be the most famous UFO incidents of the 21st Century (at least so far).

Among the numerous instances of worldwide trauma, dystopian experiences, and bizarre occurrences in the year 2020 was something that UFO believers and enthusiasts have been eagerly anticipating for almost a century. Tucked in between the rapid onset of the COVID-19 pandemic and fearmongering about "murder hornets" was something truly remarkable—the United States military making an official confirmation of not just one but *several* UFO-related incidents.

The incidents in question were two separate encounters between U.S. Navy personnel and UFOs—or, to use the current terminology employed by the United States government, "Unidentified Aerial Phenomena," or *UAPs*. Of course, the Pentagon's hand *was* forced somewhat by the surreptitious leaking to several videos of the incidents. Given that these videos were taken by cameras aboard U.S. Navy aircraft and often featured clear commentary by U.S. Navy pilots, the Pentagon would have had something of a hard time directly denying their authenticity. The three videos were initially published in 2017 by *The New York Times*, under the deceptively benign titles "FLIR," "GIMBAL," and "GOFAST."

The first incident that was revealed in these leaks occurred in 2004. In November of that year, the U.S. Navy aircraft carrier USS *Nimitz* and its attached strike group were conducting training operations off the coast of Southern California in preparation for an eventual deployment into the Persian Gulf. However, the first two weeks of November brought somewhat mystifying and concerning developments to the group. One of the strike group's attached ships—a guided-missile cruiser called the USS *Princeton*—began tracking what seemed to be a strange object on its radar. This anomaly would initially appear high in the sky above the strike group, usually at an altitude of around 80,000 feet. This was well above the normal flight altitude of most commercial airliners or even most military aircraft. But, as if that wasn't strange enough, the *Princeton's* radar would then catch the object abruptly descending towards the sea at an incredible speed, then coming to an almost immediate halt at an altitude of around 20,000 feet.

Throughout this two-week period, Princeton apparently got several such readings on its radar. Some of them indicating what appeared to be a single airborne object, and some possibly indicating a group of such objects moving in a cluster. A few of the readings seemed to indicate the objects were hovering in a stationary position in the air, or else moving much more slowly than the speed that most aircraft need to maintain in order to remain airborne. Additionally, these readings were also confirmed by the radars of several other ships within the strike group, indicating that they were not merely the result of a glitch in the *Princeton's* radar system.

The extreme altitude, speed, and manoeuvres of this unidentified aerial phenomenon would place it beyond the limits of even the most advanced aerospace technology known to the United States Navy at the time. What's more, the extreme speeds and abrupt stops that were indicated on radar would have produced G-Forces that would likely damage or destroy even the hardiest of aircraft and most certainly kill any person or living creature on board. Still, despite these strange radar readings, nothing came of the report for the first two weeks of November, and so nothing was done about it. At least, initially.

That, however, changed dramatically on November 14. On that day, a group of F/A-18 Super Hornets had taken off from the *Nimitz* to engage in a routine training exercise. During the exercise, however, the carrier group's radars once more picked up the strange phenomenon in the air nearby. Now, with F/A-18s already airborne, the group of jet fighters was diverted from their training exercise to attempt to get visual contact with whatever was appearing on the radar and possibly intercept it if need be. The squad of F/A-18s, led by pilot and commanding officer David Fravor, did not have to wait long to come across the anomalous aerial object. Recounting the incident years later, Fravor said he initially saw some kind of "disturbance" in the ocean, which appeared to be some sort of large object just under the surface. In the air above the disturbance, however, Fravor and the other pilots quickly saw what they described as a "white and oval" object, which Fravor later estimated to be around 40 feet long.

While the larger object under the ocean may simply have been one of the submarines attached to the carrier group, the airborne object hovering over it was not quite as easy to identify. As Fravor piloted his F/A-18 down towards the object to get a closer look, the object, appearing to recognize the presence of potentially hostile interlopers, suddenly began to ascend skyward in an almost mirror image of Fravor's trajectory of descent. Though Fravor and the other pilots in his group attempted to get closer, the object continued to flee at an astounding speed, eventually disappearing from view entirely.

As this group of F/A-18s had only been dispatched as part of a training exercise, none were equipped with functional weapons or reconnaissance technology. Given that this object, based upon its motions in response to the approach of the jet fighters, seemed to have some kind of intelligent control, Fravor's squadron was recalled back to the *Nimitz*. In their place was dispatched another group of F/A-18s, this one fully armed with weapons and surveillance systems in an attempt at a full interception of whatever this object may be. Lt. Commander Chad Underwood, leading this group of F/A-18s, was equipped with a Forward-Looking Infrared camera on his plane. This piece of high-tech surveillance equipment, commonly known as *FLIR*, later gave its name to the video that it would subsequently take, and which would eventually be leaked to *The New York Times* years later. Underwood, like Fravor, eventually encountered the same aerial object, or at least a similar one, flying at high speed over the ocean. This time, however, Underwood was able to capture *FLIR* video of the object. The video itself shows what Underwood described as a "Tic Tac" shaped object, seemingly white in colour, flying within proximity to the strike group.

    Underwood and his group eventually lost sight of the object. However, from the video that he took, a few things became apparent about this unidentified object. One, the object, despite its high speed and impressive aerial manoeuvres, did not appear to have any obvious source of propulsion, as no such heat patterns were detected on the infrared camera. Two, though the camera did not pick up a heat signal from a clear propulsion source, it *did* pick up smaller heat patterns from the air around the object. This would indicate that the object was, in fact, solid, as the friction between it and the surrounding air would cause a sudden increase in temperature. Thus, the phenomenon cannot be explained away as a mere meteorological occurrence such as a sudden temperature inversion or something like ball lightning.

    The next incident revealed by the *Times* would not occur until over a decade later. However, as with the *FLIR* incident, the next two videos also involved a U.S. Navy aircraft carrier strike group. In 2014 and 2015, the aircraft carrier USS *Theodore Roosevelt* and its attached strike group were operating in the Atlantic Ocean, possibly off of the eastern coast of Florida. Though details of this incident are somewhat less clear than those from the earlier *Nimitz* encounter, a similar story seems to have unfolded. Radar from ships attached to the carrier group picked up strange objects on radar, seeming to achieve speeds and manoeuvres that went beyond those of any known aircraft. Jet fighters from the *Theodore Roosevelt* were eventually dispatched to try and intercept these objects and potentially take defensive action if the objects showed themselves to be any kind of threat to the ships. During these subsequent encounters, Navy aircraft captured two more videos of what the military has officially termed "Unidentified Aerial Phenomena," or *UAPs*. These two videos, which were leaked to *The New York Times* alongside the earlier "FLIR" video from 2004, have been called "GIMBAL" and "GOFAST." Both videos, as with the "FLIR" video, show a "Tic Tac" shaped object flying at high speeds over the ocean. More significantly, these two videos also contain audio of the pilots themselves, who can be heard excitedly commenting on the strange speed and motions of the object.

Of course, as with most incidents of this nature, the United States Armed Forces were less than forthcoming with information pertaining to these incidents. At least, initially. However, their hands were eventually forced, in a way, by their own inaction. Between 2007 and 2012, incidents in which U.S. military personnel encounter seemingly unexplainable objects in the skies were investigated by the Advanced Aerospace Threat Identification Program (AATIP), an unpublicized (but not classified) program within the U.S. military to investigate potential UFO encounters and determine if they may represent a specific threat to U.S. national security. Prior to its dissolution in 2012, the program was overseen by former Army counterintelligence officer Luis Elizondo. However, Elizondo found himself growing frustrated with the Pentagon's apparent lack of interest in the findings of the AATIP program, including the potential threat posed by incidents of the kind recorded in the "FLIR," "GIMBAL," and "GOFAST" videos. Thus, in

2017, Elizondo formally resigned from the military, but not before leaking the three videos to the media.

Now caught in a bind, the Pentagon was forced to take the unprecedented move and confirm, for the first time, the veracity of alleged encounters between U.S. military personnel and UFOs. In 2020 and 2021, Pentagon spokespersons officially acknowledged the legitimacy of all three videos, and even released their own versions to the press. Though this announcement was somewhat overshadowed by the ongoing COVID-19 pandemic, it nonetheless did generate a notable degree of attention from the media and the public at large. It also resulted in a greater degree of legitimacy of the question of UFOs within the broader landscape of American politics. Prior to this announcement, politicians who breached the subject of UFOs were few and far between for somewhat obvious reasons. This is not to say that *no* members of Congress pushed for greater investigations into observations of unknown aerial objects. For example, Senator Harry Reid, whose own state of Nevada houses the infamous Area 51, had for years pushed for greater funding and transparency on UFO investigations. In fact, it was his actions in Congress that led to the creation of the AATIP program in the first place.

However, now with "official" Pentagon confirmation of UFOs to point to, members of Congress grew a bit bolder in recognizing investigations into such unknown aerial phenomena as legitimate political actions. By 2020, Virginia Senator Mark Warner and Florida Senator Marco Rubio—the Chairman and Ranking Member of the Senate Intelligence Committee, respectively—both released statements demanding more comprehensive "official" information from the Pentagon on the issue. The result was a Pentagon report entitled *Preliminary Assessment: Unidentified Aerial Phenomena*, which was released to the public on June 25, 2021.

The report was officially compiled by the United States Office of the Director of National Intelligence, based on previous investigations by the Unidentified Aerial Phenomena Task Force, the Office of Naval Intelligence, and the FBI. On the surface, the report (at least, its public form) did not contain any Earth-shattering revelations. The report notably did *not* announce any verified contact between the U.S. Military and alien lifeforms, spacecraft, or technology. Nor did the report disclose any significant advancements in U.S. aerospace technology that would explain the extreme movements and seemingly impossible propulsion of the aerial phenomena observed in the videos.

However, the report *was* intriguing for a number of more subtle reasons, not least of which for its lack of clear *refutation* of the notion of extra-terrestrial or interdimensional beings visiting our world. The report, on the surface, compiled a list of the various UAPs that had been investigated by relevant bodies and grouped them into five distinct categories. The first two categories were "airborne clutter" (i.e., birds, balloons, recreational drones, and other random pieces of trash blowing through the sky) and "natural atmospheric phenomena" (i.e., temperature inversions, clouds, ice crystals, and other random meteorological occurrences that could show up on radar). The second two categories describe more advanced aerospace technology, with one category for experimental aircraft being deployed by the U.S. Military itself or private U.S.-based contractors, and another category for "foreign adversarial systems," or aerial crafts sent into U.S. airspace by a foreign power (such as China or Russia) or a non-governmental group. These categories would describe potential aircraft that would be at the far cutting edge of human aerospace technological capabilities—but still, nonetheless, of Earthly origin.

And then comes the fifth and final category, which is concisely labelled "other." While this final category ostensibly serves as a simple catch-all for any UAP that does not easily find an explanation in any of the other categories, its vague and somewhat ominous connotations did pique the interest of both UFO believers and UFO sceptics when the report was released. For its own part, the report summarized this category with a strangely open-ended description: "Although most of the UAP described in our dataset probably remain unidentified due to limited data or challenges to collection processing or analysis, we may require additional scientific knowledge to successfully collect on, analyse and characterize some of them."

Regardless of the particular stance on the question of UFOs, one must note that this report in and of itself is merely a *preliminary* report. In other words, the investigation into recent UFO/UAP sightings by the U.S. government and military is very much ongoing. It also should be noted that the version of the report released to the public was *not* the entirety of the report as it was compiled for Congress. Much in the full report remains classified. And while these classified sections likely—for the most part—involve U.S. weapons systems and aircraft that are still in developmental stages, the possibility of further, more significant revelations regarding unearthly visitors to our planet remains simmering just below the surface.

The rise and evolution of the UFO phenomenon throughout the 20th Century provided us with some of our most lasting cultural touchstones by which we understand our place in the universe. Names like *Roswell*, *Area 51*, and *Project Bluebook* are etched into our collective consciousness and may serve as either an escape from the dull acrimony of earthly reality or else a foreboding corollary of our darkest fears. And yet, the first two decades of the 21st Century have shown us that UFOs, whatever they may be, are not a mere relic of the Cold War. And now, with more and more credible sightings seeming to accumulate every year and with renewed interest from the highest authorities in government and the military, the issue seems far from laid to rest. Who, then, can say what the rest of the century will bring us?

References

Chapter 1: Amy Lynn Bradley, Disappeared 1998

https://www.fbi.gov/wanted/kidnap/amy-lynn-bradley

https://www.newspapers.com/clip/21146961/the-akron-beacon-journal/

https://historydaily.org/amy-lynn-bradley-disappearance-everything-we-know

https://www.cruiselawnews.com/2017/03/articles/disappearances/fbi-releases-new-video-regarding-amy-lynn-bradley-who-disappeared-from-rhapsody-of-the-seas/

Chapter 2: Brian Schaffer, Disappeared 2006

https://www.fbi.gov/wanted/vicap/missing-persons/brian-shaffer

https://614now.com/2019/news/unsolved-ohio-the-bizarre-disappearance-of-brian-shaffer-from-ugly-tuna

https://www.nbcnews.com/id/wbna12689476

https://www.dispatch.com/story/news/local/2021/03/29/brian-shaffer-disappearance-photo-shows-how-osu-student-may-look-now/6995317002/

Chapter 3: Jodi Huisentruit, Disappeared 1995

https://globegazette.com/news/local/search-for-jodi-huisentruit-continues-years-later/article_ccb4f1f6-bf83-5c06-835c-3d27daeff8e0.html

https://iowacoldcases.org/case-summaries/jodi-huisentruit/

https://www.kaaltv.com/iowa-news/the-search-continues-to-find-jodi-huisentruit-26-years-after-her-disappearance/6154810/

Chapter 4: Ben Needham, Disappeared 1991
https://www.bbc.com/news/uk-england-37676268

https://news.sky.com/story/ben-needham-mother-vows-to-continue-search-for-son-30-years-after-his-disappearance-12361905

https://www.yorkshirepost.co.uk/news/crime/ben-needham-30th-anniversary-family-make-heartbreaking-plea-for-the-truth-on-his-disappearance-3320342

https://www.youtube.com/watch?v=JFzk6UvyVc8

Chapter 5: Renata Antczak, Disappeared 2017

https://www.hulldailymail.co.uk/news/hull-east-yorkshire-news/missing-renata-antczak-police-statement-2793508

https://www.bbc.com/news/uk-england-humber-40300291

https://www.mirror.co.uk/news/uk-news/dentist-whose-missing-wife-subject-21026407

Chapter 6: Rebecca Coriam, Disappeared 2011

https://www.theguardian.com/uk/2011/nov/11/rebecca-coriam-lost-at-sea

https://www.liverpoolecho.co.uk/news/liverpool-news/10-unanswered-questions-over-mystery-17441647

https://www.bbc.com/news/uk-england-manchester-34659505

Chapter 7: The Incident at Dyatlov Pass

https://ermakvagus.com/Europe/Russia/Cholat-%20Syachil/Kholat%20Syakhl.htm

https://www.amazon.com/Death-Nine-Dyatlov-Pass-Mystery-ebook/dp/B07MSFVWS5/

https://www.nature.com/articles/s43247-020-00081-8/

https://www.nationalgeographic.com/science/article/has-science-solved-history-greatest-adventure-mystery-dyatlov

https://www.newyorker.com/magazine/2021/05/17/has-an-old-soviet-mystery-at-last-been-solved

Chapter 8: The Flannan Isles Lighthouse Disappearances

https://www.mentalfloss.com/article/70180/115-year-old-mystery-flannan-lighthouses-missing-keepers

https://www.history.co.uk/articles/the-flannan-isle-mystery-the-three-lighthouse-keepers-who-vanished

https://www.nlb.org.uk/history/flannan-isles/

Chapter 9: The Bridge at Overtoun that Calls Dogs to Their Maker

https://www.nytimes.com/2019/03/27/world/europe/scotland-overtoun-bridge-dog-suicide.html

https://science.howstuffworks.com/science-vs-myth/unexplained-phenomena/dog-suicide-bridge.htm

https://allthatsinteresting.com/overtoun-bridge

https://www.thevintagenews.com/2017/12/05/overtoun-bridge/

Chapter 10: The Voynich Manuscript

https://collections.library.yale.edu/catalog/2002046

https://www.nature.com/articles/news031215-5

https://web.archive.org/web/20050910212025/http://www.sciam.com/article.cfm?chanID=sa006&colID=1&articleID=0000E3AA-70E1-10CF-AD1983414B7F0000

https://www.newyorker.com/books/page-turner/the-unread-the-mystery-of-the-voynich-manuscript

https://nationalpost.com/pmn/news-pmn/canada-news-pmn/computer-scientist-claims-clues-to-deciphering-mysterious-voynich-manuscript-2

https://arstechnica.com/science/2019/05/no-someone-hasnt-cracked-the-code-of-the-mysterious-voynich-manuscript/

Chapter 11: The Mystifying Case of the Black Dahlia

https://vault.fbi.gov/Black%20Dahlia%20%28E%20Short%29%20/

https://www.fbi.gov/history/famous-cases/the-black-dahlia

https://www.rollingstone.com/culture/culture-features/has-the-black-dahlia-murder-finally-been-solved-198247/

https://www.theguardian.com/us-news/2016/may/26/black-dahlia-murder-steve-hodel-elizabeth-short

https://www.amazon.com/Black-Dahlia-Avenger-Notorious-Century-ebook/dp/B00U7Y5TI2/ref=sr_1_1?crid=2ZUQAZBNGQBMT&dchild=1&keywords=black+dahlia+avenger&qid=1632292061&s=books&sprefix=black+dahlia+av%2Caps%2C149&sr=1-1

Chapter 12: The Cleveland Torso Murderer
https://web.archive.org/web/20140724184549/http://www.crimelibrary.com/serial_killers/unsolved/kingsbury/index_1.html

https://www.amazon.com/Wake-Butcher-Clevelands-Torso-

Murders/dp/160635213X/ref=sr_1_2?dchild=1&keywords=james+jessen+badal&qid=1632292144&s=books&sr=1-2

https://www.clevelandpolicemuseum.org/collections/torso-murders/

https://www.cleveland.com/life-and-culture/erry-2018/10/55d2b5ea596983/clevelands-infamous-torso-murd.html

https://www.mentalfloss.com/article/632096/cleveland-torso-murderer-unsolved-serial-killer

Chapter 13: The Infamous Hinterkaifeck Murders

https://allthatsinteresting.com/hinterkaifeck-murders

https://www.mentalfloss.com/article/502044/chilling-story-hinterkaifeck-killings-germanys-most-famous-unsolved-crime

https://www.ranker.com/list/hinterkaifeck-farm/cat-mcauliffe

https://defrostingcoldcases.com/case-month-hinterkaifeck/

Chapter 14: 21st Century UFO Sightings

https://abcnews.go.com/US/story?id=92798&page=1

https://www.grunge.com/234728/the-unexplained-2001-ufo-sighting-over-the-new-jersey-turnpike/

https://www.chicagotribune.com/redeye/ct-redeye-xpm-2013-03-20-37880251-story.html

https://www.npr.org/templates/story/story.php?storyId=6707250

https://www.npr.org/2008/01/16/18146244/dozens-claim-they-spotted-ufo-in-texas

https://abcnews.go.com/GMA/story?id=4142232&page=1

https://www.cnn.com/2008/US/01/23/stephenville.aliens.irpt/index.html

https://www.navair.navy.mil/foia/documents

https://www.nytimes.com/2017/12/16/us/politics/unidentified-flying-object-navy.html

https://www.defense.gov/News/Releases/Release/Article/2165713/statement-by-the-department-of-defense-on-the-release-of-historical-navy-videos/

https://www.nbcnews.com/news/us-news/navy-confirms-videos-did-capture-ufo-sightings-it-calls-them-n1056201

https://www.cbsnews.com/news/ufo-military-intelligence-60-minutes-2021-05-16/

https://www.dni.gov/files/ODNI/documents/assessments/Prelimary-Assessment-UAP-20210625.pdf

https://edition.cnn.com/2021/06/27/politics/ufos-uap-extraterrestrial-life/index.html

Printed in Great Britain
by Amazon